GIN

A TOAST TO THE MOST AROMATIC OF SPIRITS

GERALDINE COATES

PRION

CONTENTS

INTRODUCTION

Gin has led a long and interesting life. Descended from the alchemist's laboratory, it first made its presence felt at the dawn of European commercial distilling when the marriage of grain spirit and juniper was celebrated in the Low Countries. It saw action as the "Dutch Courage" given to steady nerves in battle and it accompanied William of Orange to the British throne in the Glorious Revolution of 1688.

Gin has had its ups and downs and the infamous 18th-century Gin Craze was undoubtedly a low point in its history. But gin escaped the slums of London and, in the 19th century, was transformed by London's gentlemen distillers into London Dry. Thus began its meteoric rise to become one of the world's great spirits – helped by the gin-drinking habits of the British Raj and its adoption as the drink of choice for the jazz babies of the Roaring Twenties.

Currently there is another Gin Craze quite different from the first: driven by creativity, new brands emerge it seems almost weekly, new flavours are experimented with and a whole new generation has fallen in love with gin. Gin has regained its rightful place as the star of a new golden age of cocktails.

Gin is in and this book is designed to help you find out more about gin: its fascinating history, how it's made, the best gin brands and new ways of drinking our favourite spirit.

Cheers!

Geraldine Coates
2015

EARLY HISTORY

Distilling to make alcohol goes back to the dawn of time but sadly we have very few names and almost no pack-drill. The earliest recorded distillers were probably the Babylonians who, in the second millennium BC, used clay pots to extract small amounts of distilled alcohol through natural cooling for perfumes.

THE FIRST DISTILLERS

Eight centuries before Christ, the Chinese were making *sautchoo* from fermented rice alcohol, the Tatars were producing *arika* from fermented mare's milk and the Singhalese were distilling *arrack* from coconut toddy.

In around 300 AD there began to be written records of distillation – notably those of Zosimos of Panopolis who described the techniques of the fabled alchemist Maria the Jewess, believed to have invented distillation. For centuries alchemy and distillation were inextricably linked in the quest to find the "philosopher's stone", a legendary substance believed to be capable of turning base metals into gold and an elixir of life to achieve immortality.

The European tradition of distilling in an alembic still to make potable spirit almost certainly descended from the writings of Arab alchemists who had translated the earliest Greek and Roman texts. Jabir Ibn Hayyan (721–815 AD), aka Geber, in particular is credited with perfecting the alembic still, which was a crucial tool in his constant scientific experimentation. (The words al-embic and al-kohol are Arabic.)

RIGHT: *The first alembic still is reputed to have been in use in Alexandria in the 1st century AD. Early stills were usually made of earthenware or brick but although the design is crude the basic principles hardly differ from the technology of modern stills.*

In the ninth century we find Rhazes, an Arab physician, detailing the use of distilled alcohol as a medium for medicinal herbs and berries. During the Moorish occupation of Spain, Arabic scientific and medical knowledge spread throughout southern Europe via the great monastic houses, then the only centres of learning and knowledge.

In the 11th century, the Benedictine monks at the famous medical school of Salerno in Italy drew on the records of Greek and Arab scholars to create medicines based on combining spirit with various herbs, spices, berries and roots. The Salerno monks specified the uses of these natural remedies and described them as being made with *aqua ardens* (burning water, ie spirit) in the *Compendium Salerni*, one of the first medical reference books. Sadly, they wrote their production methods in code, so there are no surviving recipes. But it is almost certain

BELOW: *The rebirth of European distilling took place in the kitchens of mediaeval monasteries.*

that, because juniper grows so rampantly all over Italy, they would have developed a juniper remedy, particularly as juniper was used widely in the treatment of kidney and bladder diseases. So the most likely candidate as the first producer of a proto-gin appears to be an anonymous monk in the kitchens of a Benedictine monastery in about 1050.

Arnold de Villa Nova, a 13th-century alchemist who taught at the universities of Montpelier and Avignon, was instrumental in spreading the knowledge too. He is credited as the Father of Distilling and wrote in his *Boke of Wine* of the distillation of wine into *aqua vitae* and its subsequent flavouring with various herbs and spices. His description, meaning the water of life, has entered every European language: *eau de vie* in French, *agua ardente* in Italian, *usquebaugh* in Gaelic (from whence comes "whisky").

The rebirth of European distilling took place in the kitchens of mediaeval monasteries and great noble houses and it was almost exclusively concentrated on the manufacture of medicinal cordials and liqueurs. *Aqua vitae* itself was considered to be of great therapeutic value and it was noticed that the rich who drank more freely of it were healthier and lived longer. It took a few more centuries for people to realize that water and milk, the drinks of the poor, were major carriers of disease. Small-scale industries grew up, some of whose products still survive – Benedictine for example or Chartreuse, originally an "elixir of long life", which has been continuously produced at the same location since 1605.

In mediaeval Europe a stillatory (a small distillation device) was a standard piece of kitchen equipment and domestic duties included the production of aromatic cordials and liqueurs to be drunk as tonics. Made from a wine spirit, many of them would have included juniper and indeed recipes for juniper cordials survive.

Evidence that knowledge of juniper-based medicines had reached the Low Countries comes in 1269, when Flemish poet Jacob van Maerlant te Damme wrote about them in *Der Naturen Bloeme*, a natural history encyclopaedia. Later, Antoine de Bourbon, a French aristocrat, invented another

proto-gin. Made from a distilled spirit of wine mixed with juniper berries, it became known as "the wine of the poor".

Tantalizing though these glimpses into gin's origins are, we are still far removed from a true gin – that is, a grain spirit flavoured with juniper. These juniper-flavoured drinks were based on a distillation of wine. But in the cold, dank, vineless climates of northern Europe, it was a different story…

ABOVE: Juniper berries had long been used for medicinal purposes before their appearance in the first "gins".

DISTILLING WITH GRAIN

By the 14th century it was generally realized that potable spirits could be made from local crops such as potatoes, rye or barley. At the same time distilling was no longer the sole preserve of the dabbler, the scholar, the scientist or the medicine man. Ordinary people discovered it, firstly as a way to make use of an abundant harvest in times of plenty and secondly as a foolproof method of mitigating the harshness of lives that were all too often nasty, brutish and short. From now on, therefore, it begins to be possible to chronicle

the evolution of European spirits from cottage industries to proud national symbols – vodka in Russia and Poland, whisky in Scotland and Ireland, brandy in France and, importantly for this story, genever in the Low Countries.

In the Low Countries, an area that encompassed modern-day Holland, Belgium and parts of northern France, *brandewijn*, meaning "burnt wine", became the catch-all term for all kinds of spirit. Excise records from 1492 indicate that substantial quantities of grain spirit made from local rye were already being produced and commonly called *Brandewijn*.

GRAIN MEETS JUNIPER

From the early 1500s, numerous records exist of the regulations and taxes imposed on distilleries that were making this new-fangled grain spirit. Constant experimentation was carried out to find a way of masking the fusel oil flavours of *brandewijn* to make it more palatable. Juniper combined well with it, particularly when sweetened with sugar. It also grew everywhere and was considered to be restorative and life-giving. And so genever, from the Dutch word for juniper, came into being. It was a marriage of the tradition of making alcohol from crops in the field to drink for pleasure and the monastic tradition of experimenting with different ingredients to create medicines.

Dr Sylvius de la Boe, Professor of Medicine at Leiden University from 1658 to 1672, is often credited with being the first to combine juniper and grain spirit and call it genever. This is wrong. For a start, his dates are almost a century out. Secondly, it has become increasingly obvious that no single individual invented genever in the same way that no one person invented vodka or whisky.

According to the National Jenever Museum of Belgium genever/jenever was first produced in Flanders in the 13th century. The very first recorded mention of genever as a distilled beverage flavoured with juniper was in 1552, in a book called Een Constelijck Distileerboec by Antwerp-based Philippus Hermanni. That's not to say there are no other recipes yet to be found and no doubt diligent historians will keep looking.

One reason why genever was soon established as the national drink of the Low Countries was that a national distilling industry and a huge export trade rapidly developed. Between 1500 and 1700, distilleries were established in every town and distilling became as distinctively Dutch as cheese-making.

Foreigners claimed that it was the foul climate of the Low Countries that made drinking so much a part of life but there were other reasons. The innate Dutch inventiveness and love of experimentation meant that there was virtually no ingredient that they would not distil into strong drink. Crucially, there was a surplus of the ingredients distillers needed. The Dutch had a vast maritime empire based on trade and, every hour of every day, the ships of the East India Company (the famous

Vereenigde Oost-Indische Compagnie or VOC) unloaded precious cargoes of goods and foodstuffs from all over the world at the ports of the Low Countries.

In return the Dutch carried spirits, cognac, which they had virtually invented, as a way to transport wine in spirit form on long sea voyages, and genever, their home-grown spirit, to the ports of northern Europe, Indonesia, the Caribbean, West Africa – everywhere there was a deal to be done. In the 16th century Amsterdam became the pre-eminent port for sugar and spices and a centre for liqueur-making. Rotterdam was the grain port and Schiedam, its satellite town, became the hub of genever production. Genever is proportionately still the most-exported spirit in commercial history. By 1792, the Dutch were selling 4.2 million gallons of genever abroad annually.

BELOW: *In the 16th century the genever industry moved lock, stock and barrel out of Rotterdam, the principal grain port of the Low Countries, to its satellite town, Schiedam. In its heyday Schiedam could boast more than 400 distilleries.*

THE ENGLISH ENCOUNTER GENEVER

The English were introduced to genever during the 80 Years War (1568–1648) when the armies of France, England and Spain fought over religion, politics and territory in the Low Countries. Here, English mercenaries were introduced to the local grog, given to steady their nerves before battle. They christened it "Dutch Courage". Later even the great Duke of

BELOW: *The River Thames around London Bridge was always busy as genever importers sailed into London and delivered their goods at dozens of the city's riverside docks.*

Marlborough recommended its use "when they were going any time to engage the enemy", and great victories like Blenheim in 1704 and Ramillies in 1706 were credited to its powerful effects. When English soldiers and sailors returned to "Blighty" they usually brought their genever habit with them.

In 1570, London had become home to 6,000 Flemish Protestant refugees so already genever was not unknown in England. Indeed, thousands of gallons of Dutch genever

were imported to England in the 17th century – legally and illegally – but it was not until the end of the century that the English officially became a nation of spirits drinkers.

In England spirits had been distilled in a small way since Tudor times. Whisky production was confined to Scotland and Ireland but, because the English had always relied on cheap imports of French brandy, large-scale domestic distilling concerns had never developed at this time.

However a petition to Parliament in 1621 gives us an idea of the purpose of the English distilling industry in that it supplied "those that be aged and weak in time of sudden qualms and pangs" and the "King's ships and merchant ships for use shipboard and for the sale to foreign nations". There were almost 200 small businesses in London and Westminster making *aqua vitae* and "other strong and hott waters" for medicinal purposes. Distilling became regulated when, in 1638, Sir Theodore De Mayerne, a physician and alchemist, founded the Company of Distillers. It received a Royal Charter that gave a monopoly to members of the Company to distil spirits and vinegar in London and within a radius of 21 miles. The Company codified the required methods of distillation and the rules governing its practice. This monopoly and the quality standards that accompanied it were swept away in the Distilling Act of 1690 but returned later. Today the Worshipful Company of Distillers is still one of the City of London's most important institutions, engaged in protecting distillers' interests and in many trade and charitable activities.

Although there were sporadic outbursts of alarm at spirit-drinking amongst young men about town, strong water was still mostly medicinal – indeed, it was common practice to carry a supply of spirit in small flasks for use as a restorative. Samuel Pepys, a renowned social commentator, noted in

ABOVE: *Samuel Pepys (1633–1703) was an English naval administrator and MP who is now most famous for the diary he kept in which he chronicled the great events of his time such as the Great Fire of London in 1666.*

his diary entry of 10 October 1663 that "Sir W. Batten did advise me to take some juniper water ... strong water made of juniper" as a cure for the indigestion that was plaguing him. The fact that Pepys, well-known man of fashion and *bon viveur*, considered these "hot waters" as purely therapeutic is a reliable sign that they had not yet evolved into social drinks. As the century wore on, we see spirits and what were known as distilled cordial waters, the forerunners of liqueurs, begin to be transformed from medicine into drinks that were drunk for pleasure. After all, what worked as a cure for indigestion could then easily be offered as a *digestif* after a large meal.

GIN'S GLORIOUS REVOLUTION

What changed things was the arrival of a Dutchman on the English throne. In 1688, the year of the Glorious Revolution, the unpopular Stuart king, James II was replaced by the Protestant William of Orange who was married to Mary, James's daughter. The most immediate result was that everything Catholic and French was out, all things Protestant and Dutch were in.

A powerful cabal of landowners, many of whom had helped William to the throne, pushed the 1690 Distilling Act through Parliament. It was to have an enormous impact on the drinking habits of centuries by introducing legislation to ban French imports of wine and brandy and encouraging the distillation of "good and wholesome brandies, *aqua vitae* and spirits, drawn and made from malted corn".

The Act created the economic conditions for an English distilling industry. Farmers and landowners were delighted because it enabled them to sell surplus and substandard crops at a profit. It also negated the monopoly of the Worshipful Company of Distillers. From now on distilling was open to all, once a public notice of the intention to distil had been posted for at least 10 days.

Other strategic pieces of legislation gave a further boost to the development of the distilling industry. The raising of taxes on beer in 1694 made spirits cheaper than beer for the first time, whilst the 1720 Mutiny Act excused tradesmen who were distillers from having soldiers billeted on them – even more of an encouragement.

ABOVE: *The succession of a Dutchman, William of Orange, to the English throne secured a place for gin in the national drinking culture.*

There was clearly now every reason for distilling in early-18th-century England to flourish, but why that new industry should have flung itself so wholeheartedly into the production of gin, or Geneva as it was then called, is not so obvious. At its most simple England's headlong rush into the years of madness of the Gin Craze was, like many other crazes, fuelled by fashion and greed.

The fashion for drinking Geneva was led by King Billy and his mainly Dutch court. As the poet claimed: "Martial William drank Geneva yet no age could ever boast a braver prince than he …" In the new, more egalitarian, more democratic England that had emerged from the Bloodless Revolution, drinking this new spirit was a sign of patriotism and Protestantism. It became a symbol of a desire to set aside the old religious and political arguments which had dominated the century, itself now drawing to a close, and to embrace the new wherever it could be found.

Gin's dual nature was manifest from the start. The conditions were already established in which virtually anyone who wished could climb on board the distilling bandwagon and profit from the new fashion for drinking spirits. What could be more of a gift to greedy, unscrupulous distillers than a heavily sweetened drink in which the strong flavour of juniper and other spices could hide a multitude of sins? The stage was set.

LEFT: King Billy, *as William III of England and William II of Scotland was known, reigned from 1689 to 1702. His wife, Queen Mary, died in 1694.*

OVERLEAF: *One can see how gin came to be called Mother's Ruin in these sarcastic descriptions of drunken "Sweethearts and Wives" by the caricaturist Richard Newton.*

May we have in our arms what we love
in our hearts No Tax upon Gin!
Here we go up up up.....and there we go down, down,
down!

Bless me is that the Sun or the M--
sat above there!

The Cunning Woman

I'm a little sickish or so, but no matter
I've given Sal her gruel!—She drink Gin
with me! blast me she could as soon swallow
the fat Landlady!

St Giles's

She's got her quantum, by jingo! She smells as s—
daisy! but no matter, I've got the blunt in the m—
from her old Goat of a Keeper. For my conscience
he will have a precious bedfellow of her to night!

Too much of a good thing!

THE GIN CRAZE

BELOW: *Hogarth's* Gin Lane *captures all that was tragic and corrupt in the wake of the unprecedented "Gin Craze".*

In 1689, English distillers produced around 500,000 gallons of *aqua vitae* mostly for medical use. Less than 50 years after deregulation, London alone produced 20 million gallons of spirits. This figure did not include the vast quantities of illegal spirit: distillers had developed crafty ways to avoid duties by keeping hidden stills and secret tanks.

Honest distillers redistilled this spirit into Dutch-style genever using proper botanicals. But most of it ended up as potent rotgut, often mixed with water and sold in quarter-pints in one of London's many dram-shops for the price of a penny.

This new spirit was called "gin", a word that was originally the upper classes' satirical nickname. Incidentally the first recorded use of the word is found in a political pamphlet published in 1714, entitled, *The Fable of the Bees, or Private Vices, Publick Benefits* by Bernard Mandeville, an Anglo Dutch philosopher, appropriately enough. In this satirical study Mandeville writes of "the infamous liquor, the name of which, derived from Juniper berries in Dutch, is now, by frequent use and the Laconick spirit of the Nation shrunk into a Monosyllable, Intoxicating Gin that charms the unactive, the desperate and the crazy of either Sex …".

By the 1720s, the streets of London were awash with cheap, noxious spirit. The slums of St Giles, an urban hell, were gin central as London's poor discovered this new highly addictive drug. This area (behind modern-day Oxford Street where Centre Point now stands) was the setting for William Hogarth's famous engraving *Gin Lane*, a visual parable on the shocking effects of the gin-mania that gripped the city. Here is pictured the slatternly mother, too drunk to notice her child is falling from her arms. Drunkards fight in the street and desperate customers queue at the pawnbrokers in search of money to buy gin. Dangling in the sky is the figure of a bankrupt who has hanged himself. Crowds storm Kilman's, the distillers. Carved above the cellar door below is the famous sign: "Drunk for a penny, dead drunk for tuppence, straw for free."

Hogarth had been inspired to make this powerful piece of propaganda by statistics such as these:

- The death rate in London, in 1723, outstripped the birth rate and remained higher for the next 10 years.

- Between 1730 and 1749, 75% of all the children christened in London were buried before the age of five.

- At one point, there were 7,044 licensed gin retailers in a city of 600,000 people, plus thousands more street vendors peddling the deadly spirit.

- Between the years 1740 and 1742, in London, there were two burials to every baptism.

- The hospices and hospitals in the city were packed with "increasing multitudes of dropsical and consumptive people arising from the effects of spirituous liquors".

- Nine thousand children in London died of alcohol poisoning in 1751.

The whole of London society was scandalized by the story of Judith Dufour, who had taken her two-year-old daughter from the workhouse, strangled her, and sold her clothes to pay for gin. It was extensively reported in the newspapers of the day and contributed to an image of the London poor as a drunken, out-of-control population. Numerous pamphlets and articles denounced gin as the ruin of family life and slowly the demand for reform became unstoppable.

Attempts began to be made to control the gin madness. They were badly thought out – like the one that decreed that only dwelling houses could sell "intoxicating liquors". The Act of 1736 caused the most controversy as it attempted to fix a licence fee of £50 for gin retailers, prohibited the sale of gin in quantities under two gallons and taxed gin at £1 per gallon. The reaction was outrage. This Act inspired poetry and pamphlets and even a long-running theatre show written by Henry Fielding.

On the eve of the Act becoming law there was a night of extreme gin madness. Mock funeral processions took place all over the country, with people carrying effigies of Madam Geneva. In London, taverns painted their punch bowls and signage black and an official funeral for Mother Gin took place in Swallow Street, just off Piccadilly, complete with a horse-drawn funeral carriage and hordes of mourners dressed in black, drinking the last legal gin in copious quantities.

But nothing much changed. In fact, sales of illicit gin – now sardonically called "Parliamentary Brandy" – soared, and in 1742 the Act was repealed.

THE GIN OF THE GIN CRAZE

The only thing that modern gin has in common with the gin of the Gin Craze is the name. Gin had many other nicknames – Madam Geneva, Ladies' Delight, Royal Poverty, My Lady's Eye-water, Kill-Grief, Cock-my-Cap, King Theodore of Corsica and Blue Lightning (because habitual gin-drinkers' faces often turned blue) – to name just a few.

The traditional way of purifying spirit by re-distillation was expensive, time-consuming and required skill, not to mention proper stills and equipment. Setting up a distillery could cost as much as £4,000, a staggering sum in those days. The bootleg-distillers in St Giles and the East End needed much quicker results. So substances like oil of turpentine mimicked the flavour of juniper berries whilst sulphuric acid, rock salt and quick lime were used to purify cheap spirit or "low wine" that had been distilled once or at the most twice. According to the anti-gin crusaders, distillers often threw in rotten fruit, urine and animal bones. Almost certainly they sneaked in hard maltum, a poisonous alkaloid frequently used by nefarious brewers to make beer more inebriating.

AN INDUSTRY IS BORN

In 1743 the government introduced yet another Gin Act. This one achieved a balance between the need to control gin production – urgent now, given that spirit production had reached eight million gallons with only around 40 gallons declared for duty – and pragmatism. Rather than trying to enforce a form of prohibition, Parliament was encouraging the far more realistic goals of control and moderation.

Spurred on by the success of this Act and a rising anti-gin crusade, Parliament passed a law in 1751, known as the Tippling Act. Only established licensed public houses could now sell gin. If credit was given to customers, sums under £1 were not recoverable in law and those in charge of jails and workhouses were specifically forbidden to retail alcohol.

By further controlling those who could sell gin and by raising excise duties to a level that would discourage the back-street boys, the Tippling Act dragged gin kicking and screaming out of the gutter. Taxes and duties on gin began to produce a valuable source of revenue for the public purse and the excise duty on spirits was raised steadily. Prices rose correspondingly and consumption fell. During the years of bad harvest between 1757 and 1760, all distillation of spirits from grain was prohibited. This had such beneficial effects on public health that there were demands that the prohibition should be permanent. The farmers protested vociferously. A compromise was reached and the duty was raised yet again.

By the closing stages of the 18th century the Gin Craze was virtually over. Ever-increasing excise duties meant gin was no longer cheap. Stricter quality controls led to the proper supervision and management of distilling and drove out the unscrupulous. This encouraged respectable companies to begin to make quality products and it is no coincidence that the rise of the great English distilling houses dates from this time.

London was the centre of the trade and, by 1790, was producing 90% of English gin. As the city with the biggest population, it had never-ending demand but there were many reasons why London was the perfect location for distillers. From its earliest times, the growth and prosperity of London were based on the fact that it had an estuary with a double tide that allowed goods to be brought up the River Thames

BELOW: *Between 1760 and 1815 London's population doubled in size as it became the first "world city".*

from the sea into the heart of the city. By the time reputable gin-distilling developed in the late 18th century, London's dockyards had doubled in size and expanded eastwards. Now London was the biggest and busiest port in the world. Tourists came from all over Europe to gaze at the Pool of London and marvel at how it was possible to cross the river by means of the ships moored there.

Thanks to the River Thames, the motorway of its time, London's distillers had easy access to the raw ingredients they needed: fruit, spices and herbs brought in by the East India Company, sugar from British colonies in the Caribbean; grain from East Anglia and Kent.

In 1794, there were around 40 distillers, malt distillers and rectifiers, in the cities of London and Westminster, and Southwark, according to one contemporary trade directory. Compare this with 50 years earlier when there were reckoned to be 1,500 in the same area with most owning less than £100-worth of equipment.

Distilling had become big business with a number of London tradespeople dependent on it for their living. A contemporary account describes them as "coopers, backmakers, coppersmiths, wormmakers, smiths, bricklayers, plumbers, all concerned in the coal trade, all employed on the land producing the corn, landlords, those that carry it to the sea or waterside, captains and masters, sailors, bargemen, corn factors, millers and all those involved in bringing in spices, seeds and sugar from abroad". Farmers, too, relied on the distilling trade as it allowed them to sell below-standard grain at a profit. It is estimated that, in the 1820s, around three-quarters of the grain on the London corn market was purchased by distillers.

Because large quantities of clean water are required in the distillation process, many distillers were located in those parts of London that were not only convenient for river transport but also close to sources of pure water. Clerkenwell, the site of an ancient and sacred spring called Clerk's Well, was a distilling hub. It was connected directly to the docks via the River Fleet, then the second-largest river in London.

The introduction of a minimum legal still capacity led to smaller firms, which did not have the resources to invest in production, being swallowed up by larger ones. Gradually the industry became concentrated into fewer hands and, by the 19th century, there were about six large distilling firms and several smaller ones, based in London producing quality products. Of these Booth's and Boord's were the largest producers and Gordon's was already prominent.

Distilling had shaken off its disreputable image. A major sign of social acceptance came when an important distiller, Sir Robert Burnett, was made Sheriff of the City of London in 1794. As the ever-waspish Boswell commented in his *Life of Johnson*, "Foreigners are not a little amazed when they hear of brewers, distillers and men in similar departments of trade held forth as persons of considerable consequence."

BELOW: *Diarist and author James Boswell was a part of the London social and drinking scene in the late 18th century.*

OLD TOM GIN

JAMES MELLOR & SON

LIVERPOOL

LONDON DRY GIN

Lord Kinross in his book *The Kindred Spirit* gives a marvellous description of gin as the "ardent spirit which rose from the gutter to become the respectable companion of civilized man". That rise was accomplished through a combination of an evolution in the drink itself together with a broader change in social conditions and attitudes towards drinking. It started in the 19th century.

OLD TOM GIN

At the beginning of the 19th century, the gin sold in barrels to retailers was often accompanied by descriptors such as "Old Tom", "Young Tom", and "Celebrated Cream Gin". What seemed to have happened over time was that, in much the same way as Hoover would later become the common name for any type of vacuum cleaner, Old Tom became the generic name for gin and later evolved into the term distillers used for sweetened gin. In the beginning, however, all gin was sweetened: first, because sugar very effectively masked fusel oil flavours in the base spirit before the invention of the continuous still allowed for a clean neutral spirit to be made; secondly, because popular taste leant towards sweetness. Old Tom was then produced around 25% ABV and was sold in drams in the gin palaces to be drunk neat in shots.

It is believed that Old Tom gin got its name from a certain Captain Dudley Bradstreet, an enterprising bootlegger. When the first spectacularly unsuccessful attempt to control gin sales was made in 1736, he acquired a property on Blue Anchor Lane and invested £13 in gin purchased from Langdale's distillery in Holborn. He set up a painted wooden sign of a cat in the window and broadcast the fact that gin could be purchased "by the cat". Under the cat's paw sign there was a slot and a lead pipe, which was attached to a funnel situated inside the house. Customers placed their money in the slot and duly received their gin. Bradstreet's business prospered until complaints about the "cat-man" became too numerous and competitors emerged. His idea was soon copied all over St Giles where people would stand outside houses, call out "puss" and when the voice within replied "mew", they knew that they could buy bootleg gin inside.

Unlikely as it seems, the story of the bold Captain Bradstreet is probably true. What is certainly true is that by the time branded bottles came in, most brands of Old Tom gin carried an illustration of a black cat.

All the distilling companies produced an Old Tom-style gin until the 1960s when, because of lack of demand,

George Cruikshank

production slowly ceased. Old Tom then became virtually extinct but it's become available again as a number of Old Tom-style gins have launched in response to modern bartenders' desire to create the authentic cocktails of yesteryear. (See *Brand Directory* on page 93 for details.)

OVERLEAF: Tom & Jerry taking Blue Ruin after the Spell is broke up, *another Cruikshank gin cartoon from 1820.*

Tom & Jerry taking Ji...

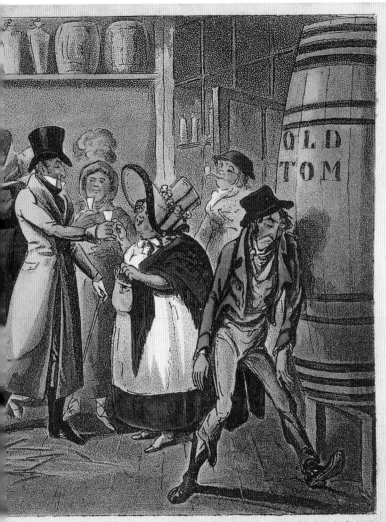

Drawn & Engraved by I.R. & G. Cruikshank.

Ruin, after the Spell is broke up.

THE CREATION OF LONDON DRY

Throughout the early 19th century, when people drank quality gin, they were usually drinking Old Tom or various types of Geneva or Hollands (all basically copies of Dutch-style genever). By the 1860s, however, heavy, sweet gin began to be displaced by unsweetened, clear gin in what came to be known as the London Dry style. "Dry" because it was unsweetened – "London" because most of the distillers making it were in London.

There are several practical reasons why this new style of gin gradually took over. First, of course, was the increasing use of the continuous still that allowed a purer, more consistent spirit to be made. Now the quality of a pure grain spirit could be enhanced with subtle flavours rather than disguised with sugar.

Sugar had arrived in 19th-century London in vast quantities at the West India Dock. Completed in 1802, it was the largest dock complex in the world, the massive £600,000 cost having been paid by the sugar merchants, plantation owners and slave traders who "invested" their profits from the thriving trade in sugar and people.

Secondly, a great disaster overtook London's distillers in the 1870s, when the impact of the dreaded *phylloxera* blight began to be felt. *Phylloxera* was an aphid infestation imported on vine stock shipped from the US to France in 1862, which destroyed most of Europe's vineyards. Consequently, brandy became almost unobtainable.

Distillers at this time made a huge variety of liqueurs using French brandy as well as gin. Cherry brandy, curaçaos, parfait amour, ginger brandy, maraschino, noyeau and others were the big sellers. Suddenly an entire income stream disappeared. Distillers realized that they had to diversify. Whilst some began to bottle Scotch and Irish whiskies as "British liqueurs", others took a long, hard look at gin as demand for it increased among sophisticated drinkers now deprived of brandy. Slowly but surely gin was crawling out of the back streets to become a drink for the affluent middle classes.

DRINKING HABITS IN THE 19TH CENTURY

Gin-drinking did not simply disappear once the Gin Craze ended and the back-street distillers disappeared. The poorest of the poor could no longer afford it but gin still provided solace and comfort to the working poor in large cities like London. Even here gin drinking was becoming more refined and one of the most popular gin drinks was purl. Originally purl had been ale steeped with herbs such as the tops of wormwood plants and other bitter herbs. By the middle of the 19th century the recipe was to mull ale with gin, sugar and spices such as ginger. It was sold by purl-men from purl-boats on the Thames and in many taverns and alehouses.

However, attitudes towards drink and drinking fundamentally changed during Queen Victoria's long reign. Throughout the previous century one thing those at the top of the social scale and those at the bottom had had in common was a love of excessive drinking. In 1773 the famous Dr Johnson spoke of a time when "all the decent people in Lichfield got drunk every night and were not thought the worse of". By Victoria's time, drunkenness was not socially acceptable amongst the upper classes. Even more importantly, the lower classes were to be actively protected from the evils of drink.

The British Temperance movement started in Preston in Lancashire in 1832 with the signing of the first abstinence pledge. Many thousands signed the pledge at mass rallies and influential people joined the cause. Although the Temperancers never had much political success in Britain, their main achievement was to drive through legislation to control when, how, and by whom alcohol could be sold, much of which was beneficial. Who for example would dispute banning the practice of selling small children "squibs" – child-size portions of gin sold by unscrupulous landlords?

Ironically the failure of the Temperancers to completely ban the sale and consumption of alcohol enshrined the right to drink in British law – encapsulated by the bishop who declared during yet another stormy licensing debate in the House of Lords, "I would rather see England free than England sober." Later, when the Liberal government sought re-election in 1874, it was rejected by voters bitter about Gladstone's capitulations

OPPOSITE: *William Ewart Gladstone (1809–98) was Prime Minister four times. He blamed the ending of his first term of office to anti-prohibitionists who had opposed his government's attempts to control the sale of alcohol.*

to prohibitionism. "We have been borne down in a torrent of gin ..." the defeated Gladstone complained.

Spirits were still seen as the problem: drinking beer by comparison was perceived as wholesome and somehow English – at least, until the more hard-line teetotallers entered the fray.

PALACES OF THE PEOPLE

One should never forget that the companion piece to Hogarth's *Gin Lane* was *Beer Street*. In *Beer Street* (reputedly sponsored by a cartel of London brewers) all was quiet, orderly and peaceful. As part of the anti-gin drive, the consumption of beer had been actively encouraged and the number of licensed beer shops proliferated. Many were dirty and ramshackle, so magistrates demanded improvements before granting and renewing licences. Beer-shop owners would often borrow money from the major brewers in order to make the necessary improvements, in return promising to buy supplies exclusively from them. And so began the "tied house" system that was to indirectly have a major effect on gin's rise to respectability.

By 1816 half the victualling houses in London were "tied" and brewers were building even more upmarket premises to draw in the passing trade. Desperate to compete, the seedy gin-shops upped their ante, transforming themselves into oases of glamour, people's palaces where ordinary folk could escape their wretched surroundings. The more sordid and squalid the neighbourhood, the more numerous and luxurious were its gin palaces. There is a contemporary description of one of these by Dickens from *Sketches by Boz* that is so evocative it deserves to be quoted at length:

"You turn the corner. What a change. All is light and brilliancy. The hum of many voices issues from that splendid gin-shop which forms the commencement of the two streets opposite; and the gay building with the fantastically ornamented parapet, the illuminated clock, the plate-glass windows surrounded by stucco rosettes, and its profusion of gas-lights in richly-gilt burners, is perfectly dazzling when contrasted with the dirt and dark we have just left. The interior is even gayer than the exterior. A bar of French-polished mahogany, elegantly-carved, extends the whole width of the place; and there are two side-aisles of great casks, painted green and gold, and bearing such inscriptions as 'Old Tom, 549'; 'Young Tom, 360'; 'Samson, 1421' – the figures agreeing, we presume, with 'gallons', understand. Beyond the bar is a lofty and spacious saloon, full of the same enticing vessels, with a gallery running round it, equally well furnished. On the counter, in addition to the usual

spirit apparatus, are two or three little baskets of cakes and
biscuits which are carefully secured at the top with wicker-work
to prevent their contents being unlawfully extracted."

The success of the gin palaces introduced the idea of drinking as
a social activity, not merely a shortcut to oblivion. The first to open
in London was probably that of Thompson & Fearon's in Holborn

BELOW: *Hogarth's*
Beer Street, *where
order, quiet and peace
preside, is the antithesis
of his apocalyptic* Gin
Lane.

BEER STREET.

Beer, happy Produce of our Isle
Can sinewy Strength impart,
And wearied with Fatigue and Toil
Can chear each manly Heart.

Labour and Art upheld by Thee
Successfully advance,
We quaff Thy balmy Juice with Glee
And Water leave to France.

Genius of Health, thy grateful Taste
Rivals the Cup of Jove,
And warms each English generous Breast
With Liberty and Love.

in around 1832. Soon they were a feature of life in industrial cities.
(In fact many fine examples remain despite the vandalism of the
1970s – the Barley Mow, the Princess Louise and the Salisbury in
London, the Cafe Royal in Edinburgh, the Horseshoe in Glasgow
and perhaps one of the most famous bars in the world – the
Crown in Belfast, owned by the National Trust which spent over
£400,000 to restore it to its original palatial glory.)

Not everyone approved and one only has to look at the drawings
of reformed alcoholic George Cruikshank, Dickens's illustrator, for
the moralists' point of view.

*ABOVE: A propaganda
envelope produced
by the Temperance
movement featuring
satirical scenes
from Hogarth and
Cruikshank's line
drawings.*

GIN'S INCREASING RESPECTABILITY

Once the principle of moderate drinking was established in law
and the stigma attached to gin-drinking in particular began to
disappear, the new essentially middle-class style of gin quickly
found middle-class audiences, particularly amongst women. In
1861 off licences to sell alcohol were granted to retailers. By
1872 the Temperance societies were up in arms about "grocers'
gin", citing cases like that of the Ipswich shop which sold
gallons of gin a week almost exclusively to women. Many of
these were genteel Victorian ladies who served gin at tea parties
from decanters labelled "Nig", coyly calling it "white wine".

*OPPOSITE: A vision of
mahogany and etched
glass, the façade of
the Prince Alfred
in west London is a
well-preserved example
of the Victorian gin
palace.*

GIN AND THE BRITISH EMPIRE

This was also the great age of colonialization when the sun never set on the British Empire. For thousands of expats serving in far-flung outposts, English gin was not just a cure for homesickness, it was a lifesaver – literally. They drank it with another new invention – Indian tonic water – to prevent malaria. When they finally came home they brought the taste for this new, sophisticated drink with them. And, if Rear Vice Admiral (rtd) Jenkins drank gin, it must be all right.

In the 19th century whilst other ranks drank the traditional Navy drink of rum, gin became the drink of officers on British Navy ships. (The same had been true a century earlier on Dutch ships where the officers drank

genever, the lower orders rum.) Wherever the Navy went they took gin, sowing the seeds of a huge export trade.

Until the mid-19th century all UK-produced gin was for the domestic market. Heavy excise duties handicapped the export trade until, in 1850, Sir Felix Booth of the Booth distilling family spent a small fortune on pushing a Private Bill through Parliament to remove excise duties on export gin. Orders poured in from every corner of the world, particularly those corners that the British had painted pink. Gordon's, for example, still have a record of a shipment to a group of Australian miners who sent their payment in advance – in gold dust. The reputation of English gin began to travel the world.

The connection between gin and the Navy remains in the "gin pennant", the green and white flag traditionally run up as an invitation to board.

ABOVE: *The British in India were the first to make the connection between gin and tonic water when they livened up their daily anti-malarial with a dash of the London Dry.*

UPWARDLY MOBILE

BELOW: *The publication of Booth's* An Anthology of Cocktails, *in which the cream of society gave their favourite cocktail recipes, firmly placed the "scene" in British culture.*

OPPOSITE: *The difference is clear – Gordon's export gin is instantly distinguished from the green of its home sales product.*

A further sign of social acceptance was that, in the 1890s, distillers began to sell gin in bottles in response to the growing demand from the off licence trade. Until then gin was sold in barrels to the retailers who would bottle it themselves for customers to take home. With bottling came sophisticated labelling and advertising, all of which promoted gin as a quality product.

In 1898 there was a large-scale reorganization of the industry. Gordon's and Tanqueray joined forces to become the major presence in English distilling. Their combined economic power was enormous and, through rationalization of their production processes and the beginnings of a marketing strategy, they raised the status of gin as a sophisticated, international drink.

This is the Gin

AS BOTTLED FOR THE
UNITED KINGDOM

AS BOTTLED
FOR EXPORT

Gordon's
Stands Supreme

THE
MODERN
AGE

⚬━━━━━◆✕◆━━━━━⚬

By the beginning of the 20th century Dry Gin was beginning to edge out the heavy, sweet Old Tom style. The main reason for this was that it worked far better in the new craze for cocktails, which had first arrived in Europe in the 1860s, brought over by Americans who imported the fashion for sweet mixed drinks.

GIN IN VICTORIAN TIMES

Although cocktails seem to be the ultimate in modernity their origins are to be found in Victorian drinks such as cups, punches, flips and slings. American-style cocktails differed from these in that they were iced. The establishment of the Wenham Lake Ice Company in the Strand in 1845 made ice commercially available in London for the first time. The first American cocktail bar opened in the 1860s behind the Bank of England and soon cocktail bars popped up all over London. The Criterion in Piccadilly opened in 1870 and grand hotels like the Savoy and Claridge's boasted American Bars with a range of cocktails based on gin.

BELOW: Gordon's takes on the cocktail.

Some Londoners disapproved. In 1863, Henry Porter and George Roberts expressed their opinion in print: "for the sensation drinks which have lately travelled across the Atlantic we have no friendly feeling ... we will pass the American Bar ... and express our gratification at the slight success which 'Pick-me-up', and 'Corpse Reviver' have had in this country". However Mrs Isabella Beeton, the domestic goddess of Victorian England, was a fan and included recipes for Mint Juleps and Gin Slings in her famous 1861 edition of *The Book of Household Management*.

Jerry P. Thomas, aka the Professor, was one of the first and certainly the greatest of celebrity bartenders. Known as the "father of the American cocktail", by the time he was 33, he was earning more than the vice-president of the United States. In 1862 he compiled *The Bar-Tender's Guide*. For the first time the oral tradition of the recipes of the first classic cocktails was committed to print. The 1876 edition included the first written recipe for the

Tom Collins, whilst the 1887 revision had one of the first recorded recipes for the Martinez, a precursor of the Martini, made with Old Tom gin and sweet red vermouth. The Professor toured Europe with his own portable bar giving demonstrations, and many European bartenders came to learn from the master.

Until the 1890s imported English Dry Gin and Old Tom gin were sold in equal amounts in the United States, but from then on Dry Gin became the preferred cocktail spirit. There, the Dry Martini and the Bronx – both Dry Gin drinks – were the most popular cocktails.

ABOVE: *"Professor" Jerry Thomas was known for his showmanship and his signature drink, the Blue Blazer, involved setting whisky on fire and throwing it dramatically between two cocktail shakers.*

PROHIBITION IN AMERICA

On 17 January 1920, the Volstead Act passed through the US Congress and Prohibition came into force. It soon turned into a re-enactment of the 18th-century Gin Craze as millions of ordinary Americans overnight became amateur distillers and professional drinkers.

Organized crime quickly moved in on illicit alcohol manufacture and smuggling as there were vast profits to be made. An entire generation of Americans became criminals in one form or another, by either going to speakeasies, distilling at home or buying bootleg booze. Not exactly the scenario envisaged when many US towns closed down their jails on the eve of Prohibition in the anticipation that, once alcohol was banned, there would be no more crime.

RIGHT: *Never had being bad been so good – ironically, Prohibition in America produced a burgeoning drinking culture that was soon to cross the pond.*

Bathtub gin was popular. It was a vile combination of industrial alcohol, glycerine and juniper oil made in large containers to which water was added via the bath tap. To make it taste better, people added fruit juices, mixers and bitters – inventing a raft of new cocktails.

English distillers had feared losing their most important export market as a result of Prohibition. In fact, the reputation of imported English gin reached new heights as, having experienced the effects of truly bad alcohol, Americans were ready to pay exorbitant sums for the "real McCoy" (reputedly named after a rum-runner operating in the Caribbean during Prohibition). It is estimated that, during Prohibition, London distilleries exported around 40 million dollars' worth of gin to the US via Canada, the West Indies and islands close to American shores. No questions were asked when requests came in that orders should be packaged so that they could float.

On 5 December 1933, the "noble experiment" of Prohibition ended, brought to a close largely by the very people who had been its most vociferous supporters. American mothers, weary of seeing their families criminalized and of the obscene profits made by gangsters like Al Capone and Dutch Schultz, led the charge to repeal the Act. Franklin D. Roosevelt had run for president on a platform that included ending Prohibition – and on the night he was elected, it is rumoured, mixed the first legal Martini in the White House for 13 years using Plymouth Gin.

America learned that drink could be a part of civilized life and, like everything else in life, only the best was good enough. After Prohibition the demand for English gin soared in the US because the reputation of London Dry Gin had never been higher.

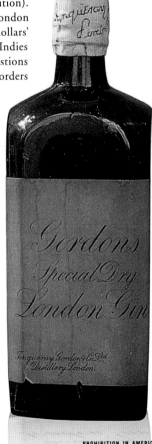

BELOW: *The effect of Prohibition on the export market was exactly the opposite of what the English distilleries had feared. Offshore sales boomed once private stocks ran out.*

COCKTAILS AND THE JAZZ AGE

The 1920s and '30s were gin's glory days. The period between the two World Wars was the age of glamour, an explosion of the new in technology, communications, fashion, the arts and popular culture. Along with fast cars, flappers in short skirts, cubist art, cinema and of course jazz, cocktails were the height of fashion.

RIGHT: *Cocktails as good as the name they bear ... Gordon's ensure their gin has its place at the heart of the new drinks craze.*

A traumatized generation who had survived the Great War simply wanted to have fun. This was a time when the old formal social order began to disappear. Dressing up for formal dinners had been abandoned and the cocktail hour was the perfect way to fill the vacuum. Cocktail parties became the rage, replacing the British custom of afternoon tea with early-evening cocktails. Reliable sources state that the cocktail party was introduced to London by an American-born hostess called Madame Alfredo de Pena in the late 1920s. Certainly from this time there is evidence of a growing cocktail culture influencing fashion, accessories, a host of gadgetry, literature, popular music and film. By now gin cocktails were simpler and new, sophisticated drinks such as the Clover Club and the White Lady were lapped up by high society.

The writer Evelyn Waugh portrayed the racy lives of young moneyed aristocrats and christened them the "Bright Young Things". Newspapers and magazines were fascinated by everything this smart set did – the first glimmerings of the modern obsession with celebrity. In his novel *Vile Bodies* Waugh describes the constant social whirl: "Masked parties, savage

BELOW: *Gin became the perfect early-evening mellower for the fast set between the wars.*

parties, Victorian parties, Greek parties, Russian parties, circus parties, parties where one had to dress as somebody else, almost naked parties in St John's Wood, parties in flats and studios and houses and ships and hotels and nightclubs, in windmills and swimming baths ... all the succession and repetition of massed humanity ... Those vile bodies." There was even a baby party with cocktails served in nursery mugs. And gin was the spur for this manic pace of life.

It was the same on the other side of the Atlantic despite Prohibition. There writers like F. Scott Fitzgerald chronicled the Roaring Twenties – a time when, as the *New York Times* put it, "gin was the national drink and sex the national obsession". Gin was Fitzgerald's favourite spirit because he believed no one could smell it on his breath, and the Gin Rickey was his favourite drink. One could easily imagine it being served at one of reputed bootlegger and mysterious millionaire Jay Gatsby's famous parties.

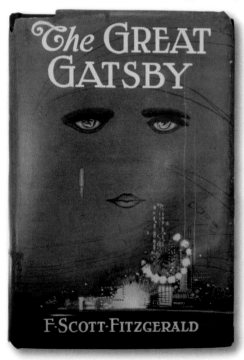

Riding the cocktail zeitgeist, distillers became much more sophisticated in their marketing. "Drinks never taste thin with Gordon's Gin" was the strapline for Gordon's advertising. At this time, Plymouth Gin and Booth's Gin were the two most famous gin brands in the world and both invested heavily in promoting their products.

Further down the social scale gin was "in", too. But cocktails never invaded the British pub, where the most popular mixers for gin were orange squash and ginger beer. A perennial favourite in working men's pubs was the Dog's Nose – a glass of gin poured into a pint of beer.

ABOVE: *An early example of Booth's advertising focused on its heritage and the reputation of Sir Felix Booth.*

POST-WAR GIN BOOM

During the Second World War, all distilling from grain in Britain was prohibited in order to conserve stocks of grain for food, and most distilled alcohol was diverted to the war effort – described by the stoical British as "Cocktails for Hitler". However, despite strict rationing, some gin was still made for the domestic market using a molasses spirit. Once the war was over, English distillers were back in action, building huge export trades and re-establishing English-made gin as the world's most sophisticated spirit.

The popularity of gin reached its apogee in the 1950s and '60s, with Hollywood stars such as Errol Flynn and Humphrey Bogart rarely seen without a gin Martini in hand. Gin was glamorous: to this day the last take of every Hollywood movie is still called the "Martini shot" as that was the signal for everyone, from big-name star to the clapperboard guy, to celebrate in style.

Gin was sophisticated and the three-Martini lunch, which President Jimmy Carter was later to condemn, was standard fare in adland's Mad Men circles. David Embury's *The Fine Art of Mixing Drinks*, published in 1948, was a guide to making cocktails at home and it seemed as though few middle-class American households did not have their own cocktail bar where mixing a Martini was the evening ritual.

Gin remained the dominant white spirit right up until the late 1960s, a time when probably around half of any cocktail list would have been made up of gin-based drinks. Then came what seemed the unstoppable rise of vodka. By the 1970s, gin was almost stagnant in terms of growth. Many traditional brands simply disappeared. Others sat unloved

BELOW: *Swashbuckler Errol Flynn was part of a hard-drinking Hollywood party crowd that included legendary drinkers such as David Niven, Peter O'Toole, Ava Gardner and Frank Sinatra.*

on dusty shelves with no investment and no innovation. Even worse, gin lost its iconic image and was perceived as old-hat and old-fashioned.

After a while, though, it was all change again. The arrival of Bombay Sapphire with its classy packaging and less juniper-dominated taste profile had attracted a whole new audience for gin. And ultimately it inspired the launch of a new wave of innovative, unusually flavoured gins both from established brands and newcomers.

BELOW: *"Of all the gin joints in all the world she walks into mine"* famously said Humphrey Bogart, the owner of Rick's bar in Casablanca.

GIN IN THE 21ST CENTURY

By the year 2000 the renaissance of gin was firmly underway, its rebirth almost entirely driven by the great revival of interest in properly made cocktails that started in the 1990s. Hard to believe now that not so long ago one could order a Martini in a relatively upmarket bar and be served a glass of red vermouth with a lump of ice! It's very different now.

At the turn of the century a new passion for food and the burgeoning of a "foodie" culture had its corollary in drink. Led by influential and knowledgeable bartenders in London and New York, a quest for authenticity and heritage would re-establish gin as the star of the cocktail scene.

Gin has always owed its success to its mixability. The reason why so many (over 7,000 and counting) cocktails are based on

gin is that what is required of a base spirit in cocktails is that it should have its own distinctive taste yet be able to blend with other flavours. Gin does this, so it's at home in the classic cocktails beloved by modern bartenders.

At the same time no two gins taste quite the same and high-quality gins with interesting new flavours inspire bar folk to come up with new drinks that showcase gin's unique personality. Many of the trends that have influenced gastronomy, such as foraging for natural ingredients and using seasonal produce, are now replicated on the menus of the best bars. The astonishing boom in craft distilling, with small independent companies unafraid to push the boundaries, has led to experimentation with new botanicals, often locally grown. Slowly but surely, gin has regained its position as the queen of white spirits.

LEFT: *Tonic water is added to a glass of gin to create the most famous and glamorous of all cocktails, the Gin and Tonic.*

MAKING GIN

At its most basic, gin is a clear, unaged alcohol, further distilled together with a selection of natural fruit and herb flavourings known as "the botanicals". Its neutral alcohol base in theory can be made out of any substance that will ferment. In practice the best gin is made from a grain spirit which is why you often see "100% Grain Spirit" prominently displayed on the label of a premium gin.

THE STYLES OF GIN

Following an EU directive of 2008 there are now legal definitions of the different styles of gin mostly designed to protect the tradition and craftsmanship attached to the London Dry style. This has given rise in turn to more rigorous definitions of "gin" and "distilled gin". This is how they work:

LONDON GIN: Does not have to be made in London, but must be made in a traditional still by re-distilling higher-quality than standard neutral alcohol (aka base spirit) with only natural flavourings (aka botanicals). No artificial flavourings can be added after distillation. Indeed, the only other substances that can be added after distillation are additional base spirit, water and a small amount of sweetening. London Gin cannot be coloured. Typical London Gins are Beefeater, Gordon's, Hayman's, Tanqueray and Whitley Neill.

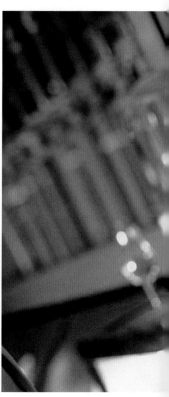

DISTILLED GIN: Made in a traditional still by re-distilling neutral alcohol in the presence of natural flavourings. Additional natural or artificial flavourings may be added after distillation, as can other approved additives such as colouring. Typical distilled gins are new-wave gins like Hendrick's Gin, the London No. 1 Gin and Martin Miller's Gin.

GIN: Often known as "cold-compounded", it's made from any type of alcohol and does not have to be re-distilled; rather, the flavourings are simply added to the spirit. The flavourings can be artificial and additional sugar, colouring and other flavourings are also allowed. No real gin-lover is seriously interested in this type of gin, but it's useful to know why some bottles of supermarket gin cost half as much as a reputable brand.

These definitions can be confusing, as they are not based on how the gin tastes. Taste is highly subjective – which is why almost every official spirit definition is dictated by production methods.

BELOW: *The purity of gin is evident in both its crystal-clear appearance and aromatic taste.*

MAKING THE BASE SPIRIT

Distillation itself is a simple process that starts with a fermented liquor containing alcohol. Alcohol's boiling point is 78.3° C whilst water comes to the boil at 100° C. When fermented liquor is heated, therefore, the alcohol in it will separate and rise in vapour form. This vapour can then be run off, cooled and collected. As it cools, it returns to a liquid form – spirit, the *aqua vitae* of the ancients.

Neutral spirit, the base for gin, is made through a process of continuous distillation in a column still also known as a Coffey still after its creator, Aeneas Coffey, a Dublin excise officer. He may well have been the first to patent the still, in around 1830, but continuous stills seem to have been developed in other locations at around the same time.

There are many advantages to continuous distillation: a lighter, cleaner, more consistent spirit can be made in large quantities, and the final strength of the spirit can be accurately specified.

Most continuous stills consist of two linked columns – the analyser and the rectifier. Alcohol-bearing liquid in the form

BELOW: *Continuous distillation at Greenall's.*

of a fermented wash is fed into the top of the rectifier. It runs down, via a pipe, to the bottom of the column and up to the top of the analyser, where it then starts to descend. Meanwhile steam enters the bottom of the analyser and rises slowly up through a series of horizontal perforated plates to heat the cool liquid. As the steam and liquid travel across the plates the alcohol, in vapour form, is separated out. It is then captured in a condenser where it cools and becomes liquid again.

The beauty of this system is that the distiller can collect the spirit at whatever strength he wants by adjusting the plates to capture the higher alcohols. Gin distillers require a neutral spirit at 96% ABV and that's exactly what they get.

Technically it would be easy enough to re-distil this on the spot but life is never that simple. Under British law, gin distillers are not allowed to produce their neutral spirit in the same location as the rectified spirit, ie gin – the result of an Act of 1825 intended to ensure unscrupulous distillers could no longer make sub-standard spirit for re-distillation into gin. So the spirit is transported to the gin distillery to be rectified or re-distilled.

Before the spirit is dispatched, samples are sent ahead for tasting. The spirit is tested again on arrival to ensure it conforms to the quality standards because, as any distiller will tell you, the spirit is the heart of a gin. Much depends on its quality and, equally, on its ability to maintain the consistency of the brand.

Given the octopus-like nature of large distilling concerns, most gin distillers source their grain spirit from sister companies within their own group of businesses. Gordon's and Tanqueray, for example, buy their spirit from a different part of Diageo's huge distilling complex in Cameronbridge, Scotland. The independent Greenwich Distillery also provides large quantities of neutral grain spirit for re-distillation.

THE SPICE TRADE

Gin is often described as "history in a glass". No wonder, when one considers the sheer diversity of berries, roots, peels, seeds and barks collectively known as "the botanicals" that are used to flavour gin.

And it's no coincidence that gin and its Dutch ancestor genever, both flavoured with juniper berries and other spices, are the national drinks of two great seafaring nations that once brought back all manner of exotica from the four corners of the world.

The trade in spices has been one of the most important shapers of European history, the cause of exploration, war and invasion for centuries. It could even be argued that the creation of great European colonial empires was mostly a by-product of the quest for domination of the spice trade, not its original purpose.

For millennia, the spice trade was controlled by Arab and north African middle-men who jealously protected the tortuous routes by which spices travelled from their places of origin in the East. They even invented such fantasies as the story that cassia grew in shallow lakes in China guarded by fierce winged animals! This sales pitch met with incredulity from the earliest times, with Pliny the Elder (23–79 AD) cynically commenting: "All these tales … have been evidently invented for the purpose of enhancing the price of these commodities."

In the 10th century, the powerful city-states Venice and Genoa prospered by importing spices directly from the Middle East and selling them at vast profit in Europe. A war between them, in 1398, saw Venice victorious and for the next hundred years the Venetian monopoly on trade routes was impossible to break. Towards the end of the 15th century, however, European navigational know-how developed dramatically and ships began to voyage further afield in the quest to reach spice-producing countries and trade directly with them. There were fortunes to be made, as nutmeg was more precious than gold and rent could be paid in peppercorns.

The Spanish royal house funded Christopher Columbus's quest to find a new route to the east by sailing west across the Atlantic in 1492. He discovered the New World but died believing he had reached China. Vasco Da Gama, the great Portuguese explorer and navigator, reached India by sailing around Africa in 1498, and set up trading posts that enabled Portugal to dominate trade with India for a century. In the early 1600s, the English and the Dutch established their own East India companies to build a network all over the Far East to trade in spices and other goods, often using brutal tactics. By the 17th century, the Dutch and the English pretty much controlled the spice trade: indeed it was often the cause of war between them. One such skirmish was resolved when England gave Holland the Banda Islands, where nutmeg grew, in return for a minor Dutch possession – Manhattan Island in the New World.

LEFT: *Navigator and explorer Vasco Da Gama opened up the trade route to India for Portugal at the end of the 15th century.*

THE BOTANICALS USED IN GIN

Botanicals make gin gin. And as soon as you walk into the room where the botanicals are stored in any distillery, you are instantly aware of how much of a debt today's drinks cabinets owe to yesterday's medicine chests. Almost all the botanicals used in gin originally had medicinal applications and many of them still do.

Each gin recipe has a different botanical mix and, whilst distillers may be prepared to talk about the botanicals they

use, their actual proportions are never revealed. One can safely presume that most gins will contain juniper, coriander, angelica, citrus and orris. And, whilst there are reputedly over 120 botanical ingredients that can be used in gin, most gins confine themselves to seven or eight, rarely more than 12. There are of course exceptions: more of that in the *Brand Directory* on page 93.

Below are the commonly found botanicals – starting with juniper, by law the principal flavouring in gin.

JUNIPER BERRIES

The juniper berries found in gin are a type of pine cone derived from *juniperus communis*, a small, coniferous shrub that grows wild throughout the northern hemisphere. Juniper gives gin its name and that instantly recognizable bittersweet taste of pine, lavender and camphor.

The medicinal applications of juniper go back to the dawn of civilization. The earliest recorded medicinal use of juniper berries occurs in an Egyptian papyrus dating back to around 1500 BC, in a recipe to cure tapeworm infestations. Juniper berries have also been found in Egyptian tombs as part of the embalming process.

BELOW: *Botanical drawings of the flora of the juniper.*

They were employed by both the Greeks and the Egyptians to ward off infections and this evolved into a belief, common throughout the Middle Ages, that the vapours from juniper berries could prevent leprosy and the bubonic plague. When the Black Death, a virulent form of bubonic plague, stalked Europe in the 14th century, killing more than one-third of the population, people even wore masks filled with juniper, breathing in its aromas to protect them from the deadly disease. Strangely this practice might actually have had some effect as juniper oil is still used in veterinary medicine to prevent fleas, and it was fleas carried by black rats that spread the bubonic plague. For humans, oil of juniper was given to alleviate kidney and bladder infections and also to treat indigestion and other digestive disorders.

The juniper used in gin is carefully sourced with the best growing wild on hillsides in Italy and Macedonia. The berries take two to three years to mature and are harvested in the autumn of their second year by beating the branches of the shrubs with sticks so that only the blue berries fall into baskets below, leaving the green ones to ripen further. After harvest the berries are spread out to dry. Once mature they develop their familiar blackish colour and are rich in aromatic oil. Because each year's crop will be slightly different, distillers regularly test a number of samples to create the exact blend of berries they require.

ALMONDS

Almond trees grow all over southern Europe. An important item of trade in the Middle Ages, almond oil is still used in medicines and skin care preparations. The bitter almond, not the sweet, is used in gin. It's also the source of prussic acid aka cyanide. First ground to release their rich oil, almonds impart a marzipan-like sweetness and softness to gin's complexity.

ANGELICA ROOT

In European folk medicine angelica has been viewed as a magical herb for over a thousand years. People made necklaces from angelica leaves to protect their children from illness and witchcraft whilst the root was believed to protect against plague. Indeed the plant takes its name from the Greek word *arkhangelos* (archangel) because of the tradition that the archangel Michael appeared in a dream to tell of its effectiveness against the bubonic plague and other infectious diseases. In Chinese medicine angelica is known as *dong quai* and prescribed for a wide variety of ailments.

Almost all gin recipes will include shredded angelica root as not only does it make Dry Gin dry, it has woody, earthy notes that help to create an integrated botanicals profile.

ANGELICA SEED

Angelica seeds are widely used in traditional folk and Chinese medicines and are also found in many liqueurs that started life as herbal remedies. In gin, their fragrant, slightly musky notes complement the taste of juniper. Distillers in the past sometimes substituted angelica seeds for juniper when the latter was hard to source, particularly because angelica grows wild throughout the UK.

ABOVE: *Angelica root was indigenous to the very northern parts of Europe, but it is now found across the continent.*

BERGAMOT PEEL

Bergamot is a citrus fruit closely related to the orange but much more sour and thus rarely grown for its juice. Instead the juice of bergamot is often used in Italian indigenous medicine to treat malaria and its essential oil is popular in aromatherapy. In the 18th century, oil of bergamot was used to flavour snuff, gin and, of course, the famous Earl Grey tea, so there is provenance here. Bergamot's instantly recognizable musky, perfumed aromas are now found in a number of relatively new gins.

CARDAMOM PODS

The word itself sums up the exoticism of the Far East and, after saffron and vanilla, cardamom is the third most expensive spice in the world. Cardamom originally grew wild in the rainforests of the Western Ghats in India. In the 19th century British colonists established cardamom as a secondary crop on coffee plantations in other parts of the subcontinent. To this day extracts of cardamom seeds are used to treat skin conditions and to aid digestion in south Asia.

Before they enter the still as part of the botanical recipe, cardamom pods are crushed to allow the full flavour of the little black seeds inside to emerge. Cardamom brings warm, spicy, aromatic flavours to gin.

CARAWAY SEEDS

A member of the parsley family, caraway is native to Europe, Asia, and north Africa but is now widely cultivated throughout the world. Caraway has been used in medicine for centuries. The Egyptians first recommended it as a digestive aid in about 1500 BC and it is still used in babies' gripe water. Caraway is also a common cooking ingredient in Germanic countries where it is used to flavour rye bread and liqueurs such as Kummel. In the still it releases sweet musk aromas not unlike liquorice.

CASSIA BARK

Cassia oil derives from the bark of cinnamon-like trees that grow in the tropics and is also known as bastard cinnamon or Chinese cinnamon.

It resembles cinnamon in flavour but is stronger and more bitter. In China cassia is considered one of the six great spices. In the west it is often used in skin care and cassia extracts used to be mixed with almond oil to make Macassar oil – a popular Victorian hair oil for men which produced an urgent requirement for anti-macassars, those little white squares of crocheted fabric that your great-aunt draped over the backs of her chairs. Cassia smells and tastes very like Dentyne chewing gum – sharp and pungent, almost medicinal.

CHAMOMILE

In Ancient Egypt chamomile was dedicated to the gods and its name comes from the Greek for "ground apple" due to its distinctive scent. In Spain chamomile is called *Manzanilla*, meaning little apple. It's also the name of a light Spanish sherry, either because chamomile may once have been used to flavour it or because the sherry is reminiscent of its aroma. In Anglo-Saxon times chamomile was used widely in beer-making until hops took over. In the Middle Ages, it was a "strewing" herb, spread on floors to make rooms smell sweeter. Chamomile is still a favourite garden herb and is used in herbal infusions and aromatherapy for its soothing and calming properties.

CINNAMON BARK

Another word that conjures up images of faraway tropical places, cinnamon is the bark of the cinnamon tree commonly found in Sri Lanka. It is used in many different types of cuisine and also in incense, massage oils and in ancient times to cure snakebites, freckles, the common cold, and kidney troubles. As in cooking, a pinch goes a long way in gin distillation as its warm, aromatic flavours can overpower.

CORIANDER SEED

BELOW: Coriander seeds have been used as a spice for more than 5,000 years and their oils as a medicine since the days of Hippocrates.

Coriander seed is one of the oldest spices in recorded history, with evidence of its use dating to over 5,000 years ago. Indeed coriander has been cultivated around the Mediterranean since ancient Egyptian times and coriander seeds were found in tombs of the 21st Dynasty. Hippocrates, the father of medicine,

first promoted its use as a medicine because its essential oil has many therapeutic properties. It's often used to cure conditions such as rheumatism, colic and neuralgia.

Coriander seeds are the second most commonly used botanical in gin and have formed part of the botanicals mix for centuries. If coriander seems an exotic ingredient for 18th-century English distillers, it should be remembered that coriander was grown commercially in southern England long before the days of global warming.

Coriander seeds look like mini-rugby balls and have a fresh, slightly spicy, sage and lemon flavour. Most distillers source their coriander from southern Europe although spicier gins like Bombay Dry and Bombay Sapphire use the more pungent coriander from Morocco.

CUBEB BERRIES

Cubeb berries are the fruit of the cubeb plant, a cardamom-like tropical vine that is a member of the pepper family. It has small white flowers that develop into tiny reddish-brown seeds or berries. Cubeb is native to Indonesia and first came to Europe via Venetian trade with the Arabs. It was once used in herbal remedies and was believed to have aphrodisiac qualities. It became a popular substitute for the vastly more expensive black pepper in the Middle Ages.

ELDERFLOWER

Elder trees are common throughout Europe and grow wild in northern temperate regions. In folklore the elder tree is a symbol of grief because the Crucifixion cross was made from its wood. It was also believed to be the tree from which Judas hanged himself. The elder has magical associations throughout Europe: it is widely believed that burning elder wood brings bad luck but that elder sprigs hung inside provide protection from witches.

Both elderflowers and elderberries are used to make wines and cordials. Elderflower has a complex and distinctive sweet smell and imparts fresh, herbal, floral notes with an acrid fruity undertone. Some describe this as the aroma of white grapes, others as cat's pee.

GINGER

Ginger is the rhizome of *zingiber officinale* and is also found in either root or powder form in many different types of cuisine. Ginger is a staple of Chinese traditional medicine and was mentioned in the writings of Confucius. It was also one of the earliest spices known in western Europe. Modern-day ginger ale and ginger beer have evolved from tavern keepers' 19th-century custom of leaving out small containers of ground ginger for people to sprinkle into their beer. In gin it imparts dry spicy flavours.

LEMON PEEL

Medicinally prized for its high vitamin C content, lemon juice was once given daily to sailors serving on Royal Navy ships to prevent scurvy. In gin, dried lemon peel – like other citrus fruit such as orange, lime and grapefruit – adds a crisp, sharp bite that enhances the juniper flavour. Some gins have a stronger citrus profile than others, particularly more traditional gins. But it's rare to find one that does not include citrus in some form.

LIQUORICE

Liquorice is grown for its long taproots, a source of natural sweetness with many medicinal qualities. It is widely used in the treatment of bronchitis and is also a common ingredient in cough medicines. Gin distillers often source their liquorice from China. It contains sugar, bitter compounds, and a substance that produces a distinctive woody, sweet flavour. Liquorice also softens and rounds out gin's mouthfeel.

MEADOWSWEET

Meadowsweet is a perennial herb that grows profusely throughout Europe, the eastern US and Canada. It has sweet-smelling white flowers and slightly almond-smelling leaves and was one of the three herbs considered to be sacred by the Druids. It's mentioned in Chaucer's *Knight's Tale* as an ingredient of a drink called "Save". In Elizabethan times meadowsweet flowers were added to herb beers and wines, and the leaves were placed into claret cups. It was also a popular strewing herb.

Meadowsweet is an excellent digestive remedy. Importantly it's also a source of salicylic acid, the basis of aspirin, the modern-day wonder drug whose name is derived from the old botanical name for meadowsweet – *spiraea ulmaria*. Meadowsweet's herbal, sweet, floral character enhances the freshness and zestiness of gin.

ORANGE PEEL

Dried orange peel is a crucial element of the botanical recipe and generally bitter or Seville orange is used rather than the sweet orange as its oil is more pungent. Bitter orange oil is also used in foods, cosmetics, and aromatherapy products. In gin it imparts fresh clean citrus notes that provide a counterbalance to the more pungent botanicals.

ORRIS ROOT

Orris is the rhizome of *iris fiorentina*, dried and ground to a fine powder. Many famous perfumes like Chanel No. 5 have orris root as their base note and it is also found in talcum powder and potpourri mixes as well as in the delicate spice mix – *ras-el-hanout* – used in Middle Eastern cooking.

ABOVE: *Dried orange peel is a key botanical ingredient in gin, but it has numerous other uses in medicine and orange oil is popular with aromatherapists..*

Orris is commercially grown in Italy. At harvest time plants of at least three years old are carefully dug up with a long-handled hoe. The rhizomes or roots are carefully broken off, and then peeled by hand. The peeled orris is scrubbed in water and left to dry on wire racks. At this stage orris is virtually odourless. It is stored for at least two years in order for it to develop its distinctive aromas. Then it is ground into a fine powder.

Aromatic and floral in itself with a hint of Parma violet, in gin as in perfume, orris acts as a miracle fixing agent, holding the volatile elements of the other aromatics together.

REDISTILLING THE BOTANICALS

Making premium gin is a craft and distillers all have their own ways of doing things, according to their own traditions and how they want their gin to taste. One major point of difference is between the "one-shot method" and the "two-shot method".

THE ONE-SHOT METHOD

Using the one-shot method the distillation process starts with charging copper pot stills with neutral grain spirit, water and the botanicals in the exact proportions of the recipe. The mix is then distilled and finally water is added to reduce it to bottling strength.

THE TWO-SHOT METHOD

Gordon's, Tanqueray and many other gins are made by the two-shot method where the still is charged with botanicals at several times the strength of the recipe. After distillation, neutral alcohol is added to restore the original proportions of the recipe. The advantage of course is that twice the amount of gin can be made in a single distillation.

STEEPING THE BOTANICALS

Some distillers steep the botanical mix in the still before distillation. It's more time-consuming and hence more expensive, but they believe it results in a fuller extraction of flavour from the botanicals. Others don't steep because they believe the botanicals become stewed. I defy anyone to spot which gins have been steeped and which not by tasting the final result, so the decision is really part of each brand's unique history and production.

THE STILLS

ABOVE: *Bombay Sapphire's botanical dry room, where the 10 botanicals are re-distilled.*

Most gin stills are onion-shaped copper pot stills exactly the same as the ones used to make malt whisky. They have elongated "swan" necks to extract the more fragrant, more volatile elements of the spirit and each will have a condenser beside it to cool the alcohol-bearing vapour back to liquid.

Copper is used in pot stills because it has the ability to remove sulphury or vegetable aromas by chemical reaction. The shape of the pot still also affects flavour, as it controls the speed at which the spirit vaporizes and begins to embed the botanical aromas. Distillers don't like to change a winning formula so, when one of the stills at the Diageo distillery (where Gordon's and Tanqueray are made) had to be replaced, the still-makers were instructed to copy the original precisely – even down to replicating dents and bashes. At the Black Friars Distillery in Plymouth, the 160-year-old still has a shorter neck than normal and a steeper curve in the lyne pipe. Why? Because that's the way it's always been, and because Master Distiller Sean Harrison believes that this design contributes to his gin's full-bodied character.

The other main type of still is the Carterhead, developed in the 19th century by the two Carter brothers who were originally employed by the renowned Aeneas Coffey. The Carterhead uses the vapour infusion method, once called "racking" – see below.

RIGHT: *A specially adapted Carterhead still used in the now rare "racking" method of distillation.*

RUNNING THE STILL

For most gins the distillation process starts when the stills are gently heated and the botanical-infused spirit begins its journey from liquid to vapour, crosses over the high swan neck of the still and returns to liquid, now gin, in the condenser. A distillation usually takes about seven to eight hours from start to finish. It's a mysterious process, with each botanical releasing its flavour at a different point in the cycle. Citrus elements emerge first, then juniper and coriander, followed by rooty botanicals such as orris, angelica and liquorice. They combine to create a glorious mélange of aromas that fill the stillroom.

ABOVE: *Master Distiller Sean Harrison believes that the shorter neck of the still at the Black Friars Distillery contributes to the full-bodied character of Plymouth Gin.*

The first and last parts of the run (the foreshots and the feints respectively) are discarded because they contain unwanted flavours – oily or off, too strong, too weak. Judging the right moment when to make the "middle cut" as it is called is critical. Once the distillation begins, therefore, the spirit in the spirit safe is constantly tested. Only when the still staff are satisfied that it has achieved the consistent flavours and characteristics of the brand is the liquid collected in the spirit receiver.

No two distillers will cut at exactly the same time or at exactly the same strength. That decision is part of the recipe and remains a trade secret. Some gins, however, are noticeably heavier with more robust aromas. This is partly because they contain larger proportions of rooty substances and partly, one supposes, because they will have been left to run longer to pick up the heavier elements of the spirit. Others are lighter in taste with more pronounced citric tones and will probably have been cut at an earlier point in the run.

The other main method of distillation is by vapour infusion. Here the botanicals are carefully layered in a copper basket at the very top of a Carterhead still, ie a pot still with a long rectifying column on top. Neutral grain alcohol alone is put into the still that is then heated. When the spirit meets the botanicals it is in vapour form and it passes slowly through the baskets, embedding the different flavours before it returns to liquid. The effect is one of "steaming" rather than the more traditional "boiling" process. Vapour infusion is used to produce all the gins in the Bombay family.

BOTTLING STRENGTH

Once distillation is complete, the gin is reduced to its bottling strength by adding water. In European law the alcoholic content of all gin must be at least 37.5% ABV (equivalent to 75 proof in North America). Most experts agree that for a gin to be considered premium it should be bottled at at least 40% ABV. Why, you may ask, when the gin will be served with a mixer or in a cocktail and so diluted considerably? Does it really matter? Yes, because alcohol carries the complex flavours of the botanicals. Below 40% ABV some of the more volatile citrus elements and aromatic top notes in gin are lost.

A word too about water. It is no accident that the 18th-century distillers made sure that their distilleries were

BELOW: *A Gordon's bottling factory. Once distillation is complete, gin is diluted back to a drinkable strength before it is packaged for sale.*

located in those parts of London noted for the purity of their water. Water accounts for an alarmingly high proportion of a bottle of gin and the water used in the distilling process and to reduce the final spirit must be exceptionally pure.

Because gin is made from wholly natural ingredients and is unaged, it contains very few of the organic chemicals known collectively as "congeners". Congeners are technically impurities but they contribute greatly to flavour. For example, over 400 different congeners have been identified in some malt whiskies. Gin generally has an average of three congeners. Research has shown that hangovers are related to the quantity of congeners in alcohol and so gin is the least likely drink to produce that dreaded morning-after feeling. That's good to know.

BRAND DIRECTORY

———◆◆✕◆◆———

The brands reviewed here are arranged alphabetically. With very few exceptions they are all premium gins, bottled at above 40% ABV. Or they are historic brands with an interesting story. This is by no means a comprehensive list as there are now literally hundreds of good-quality gins available worldwide. Although UK-made gins dominate this directory, the best US, French and Spanish gins are also included. All are widely available either in retail or on the web. For reasons of space the specific botanicals mentioned are the ones that differentiate the brand's own recipe but, unless otherwise stated, it's safe to assume each gin will contain the essential botanical DNA – juniper, coriander, citrus, orris root and angelica.

AVIATION

Aviation Gin is typical of the style of gin emerging from small American craft distilleries. Made with the Aviation cocktail in mind, it has juniper, cardamom, coriander, lavender, anise seed, sarsaparilla, and dried orange peel. Re-distilled with a 100% rye-grain neutral spirit and bottled at 42% ABV, it also has strong hints of Dutch *jonge genever*. Aviation is the ideal base for the many citrus-based vintage gin cocktails that are back in fashion again.

BEEFEATER DRY

Beefeater is the quintessential English gin created by James Burrough, a Victorian entrepreneur who had trained as a pharmacist. In 1863 he returned to London and purchased the Chelsea distilling firm of John Taylor for £400.

When the *phylloxera* blight struck European vineyards, brandy, the base spirit for many of his liqueurs, became difficult to obtain and expensive. James began to focus on gin and constantly experimented to find the perfect recipe. Today Beefeater is very much the gin that James Burrough created – a clean, bold gin with a strong juniper character and distinctive bitter orange notes. Other botanicals in the mix are almond, angelica seed and liquorice. They are steeped in a pure grain spirit for 24 hours, then run through a copper pot still. The final spirit is reduced to 40% ABV.

Beefeater is the only major international brand of London Dry Gin that is still actually made in London – in Kennington, within sight of the famous Oval cricket ground. Beefeater has long had a major export trade thanks to its clever positioning in the 1950s as a characteristically "English", not to say London, product and the use of the iconic image of the Beefeaters, the traditional warders of the Tower of London. That tradition continues and Beefeater is the gin of London as well as a leading brand found on back bars all over the world. A new visitor centre at the Kennington Distillery is now a must-go destination for gin fans. (See *Gin Places* on page 187 for details.)

BEEFEATER 24

Beefeater 24 is a super luxury addition to the Beefeater Gin family and is almost unique in incorporating leaf teas into the botanical recipe. So the core Beefeater recipe is taken to another level with the addition of a blend of Chinese green and rare Japanese Sencha teas plus grapefruit peel. On the nose, notes of citrus, juniper and the aromatic scent of Sencha are immediately apparent. In the mouth, there's a burst of citrus followed by juniper, developing into a long finish with spicy coriander. Bottled at 45% ABV, its complex flavour profile has inspired a host of new gin drinks such as The MarTEAini (see page 183).

BERKELEY SQUARE

Berkeley Square is a premium gin from Warrington-based G & J Greenall that is inspired by the herbs of an English physic garden – hence the addition of basil, sage, lavender and kaffir lime leaves. It is made using an unusual technique. First, the core botanicals and the kaffir lime leaves are left to steep in the spirit for a day alongside the other botanicals, which are wrapped in muslin. Then the still is run very slowly to capture the delicate essential oils of the bouquet garni. The green herbaceous botanicals in Berkeley Square make it an ideal gin to experiment with for interesting herbal cocktails, with garnishes like cucumber and basil.

BLOOM GIN

Another Warrington gin, Bloom is based on a triple-distilled pure grain spirit re-distilled with honeysuckle, pomelo and chamomile as well as the more "standard" botanicals. The result is a very fragrant, floral gin with an aromatic sweetness like candied fruit. The essential oils of pomelo (a close relative of grapefruit) impart a zingy citrus freshness. Ideal for a summer G and T garnished with a grapefruit slice.

BLUECOAT GIN

Named for the blue uniforms of the American militia in the Revolution, this American Dry Gin hails from Philadelphia. It prides itself on using certified organic botanicals that are re-distilled in a neutral grain spirit made from rye, wheat, barley and corn, then filtered before bottling at 47% ABV. Batch-distilled over a slow 10-hour process, the resulting liquid is exceptionally smooth, with juniper and citrus notes and faint aromas of rosehip and grapefruit.

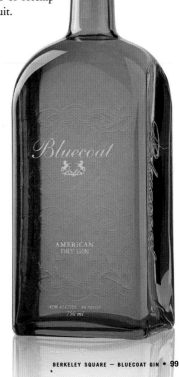

BOMBAY ORIGINAL DRY GIN

The Bombay Spirits Company was established in the early 1960s by Allan Subin, a New York-based lawyer-turned-importer of premium-quality spirits. He saw the opportunity to create a new, very British gin to challenge Tanqueray and Beefeater in the United States, and approached the Greenall's distillery with a name and a marketing plan, but without a specific taste. Greenall's came up with Bombay Original Dry based on a gin recipe found in their archives dating back to the 1760s. Made from a 100% pure grain spirit and bottled at 37.5% ABV, it's a London Dry Gin that uses eight botanicals – the traditional ones plus almonds, liquorice and cassia bark. It's distilled by vapour infusion in a Carterhead still (see page 86).

On the nose juniper, coriander and liquorice dominate. The taste is full-bodied, with piney juniper, lemon citrus and warm spice. The mighty Bacardi Martini now owns all the Bombay brands and has reintroduced Bombay Original to the UK and other European territories, which is very good news for gin fans. Even better is the decision to build a new, state-of-the-art distillery and visitor centre in Laverstoke, Hampshire, where all the gins in the Bombay family are made. (See *Gin Places* on page 187 for details.)

Bombay Sapphire is the gin that gently led the gin category out of its slump. Developed in the 1980s by Michel Roux, the driving force behind Absolut vodka, it's an immensely stylish premium gin that has attracted a whole new audience of gin-drinkers.

Michel Roux worked closely with Ian Hamilton, Greenall's head distiller at the time, to perfect the new gin, using Bombay Original Dry as the starting point. They experimented with many botanicals, test-distilling each to measure their effect on the recipe. Eventually two exotic varieties of pepper, Grains of Paradise and Cubeb Berries, were chosen. Their addition produced a gin with greater liveliness, adding unusual floral pepper and spice notes. The interaction of these two new botanicals with the others in the recipe during distillation differentiated Bombay Sapphire from the original Bombay, giving a bright juniper taste with exotic peppers on the finish. No other botanicals were added or taken away.

Bombay Sapphire is also made in a Carterhead still through infusion to pick up these more subtle spicy and fragrant aromas. Stylish packaging and a distinctive blue bottle referencing the glory days of the Raj and the famous Star of Bombay – a stunning sapphire discovered in Sri Lanka – make Bombay Sapphire instantly recognizable on every back bar. Perhaps the biggest favour Bombay Sapphire did for gin, however, is that it was the first brand to actually talk about what's inside the bottle. That alone got both bartenders and gin-lovers talking about the juniper spirit, and its success encouraged other gin distillers to experiment with innovative ingredients.

Bombay Sapphire tends to be more laid-back than many other London Dry Gins. On tasting it's slightly sweet on the nose with delicate juniper, spice and citrus flavours following on. Fresh and clean with an elegant finish, Bombay Sapphire is a barkeep's dream with extraordinary versatility in long drinks and cocktails. Speciality Sapphire serves include the Bombay and Cran and the Wet Martini where the extra vermouth enhances Sapphire's floral and spice flavours.

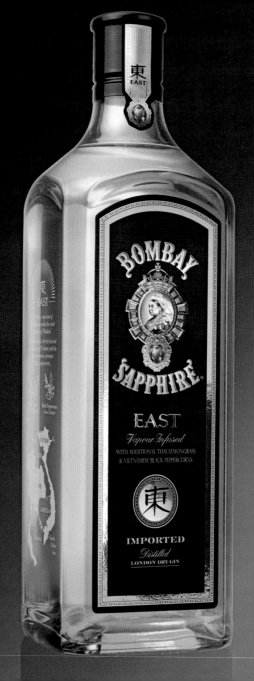

BOMBAY SAPPHIRE EAST

Bombay Sapphire East adds Thai lemongrass and Vietnamese black peppercorns to the Bombay Sapphire botanical recipe. It delivers a lovely big pepper hit alongside fragrant spice and a citrus sweetness. Bombay Sapphire East has been created with the G and T in mind, and these spicy, earthy flavours more than hold their own against even the sweetest of American-style tonic water.

BOODLES GIN

Although nowadays it is more often found at the other side of the Atlantic, Boodles is a traditional British brand dating back to 1847. It is bottled in the States at 45% ABV proof and is a high-strength, very dry gin with citrus and spice notes.

BOOTH'S GIN

Although the Booth's brand is drastically devalued nowadays and is only made in the US under licence, the name still has the power to stir the blood of gin aficionados. Word is that bottles of original Booth's High & Dry change hands on eBay for ridiculous amounts. Not surprising really when one considers that Booth's can make a good

claim to be the oldest surviving London Gin in the world. In its heyday it was constantly raved about by leading drinks writers – for example, recommended as the only gin for a Pink Gin by the great, heroic drinker Kingsley Amis.

The first recorded evidence of the firm of Booth's is a document of 1569 that mentions the Booth family as wine merchants. Presumably they expanded into gin distilling as many wine merchants did, although there is no official record until the listing of Philip Booth & Company Distillers in Clerkenwell in the 1778 *Directory of Merchants.*

In 1819 Philip's son, Felix Booth, inherited the business and began to transform Booth's into the largest distiller in the country. In 1829 Felix sponsored Captain John Ross's expedition to map the fabled North West Passage. Although that remained elusive, the expedition discovered the true position of the magnetic North Pole and Ross mapped much of the area, naming huge swathes of it after his patron. Hence one rather bizarrely finds Boothia Peninsula, Felix Harbour, Cape Felix and the Gulf of Boothia in the extreme north of Canada. Felix was also instrumental in opening up the export trade for gin.

Booth's made several London Dry-style gins. Booth's Finest was unique at the time in that it had a slightly golden colour, originally because it had been stored by accident in sherry casks. The resultant ageing improved its taste so much that it was henceforth always "rested" in sherry casks. Sadly at the time the fashion was for clear gin as that signified purity so its reputation suffered. How times change; if Booth's Finest was around today it would be hailed as an innovative breakthrough in new styles of gin. (See *Aged Gins* on page 152.)

To promote its gins Booth's commissioned *An Anthology of Cocktails* in the 1930s, which featured the cocktail choices and photographs of well-known characters such as entertainer and heartthrob Ivor Novello. One of the first known examples of celebrity endorsement in advertising, it was extremely popular and original copies are now collector's items.

After World War II Booth's High & Dry, developed specifically for cocktails, was targeted at the American market. It never quite cracked it and Booth's gins began to be passed around the great distilling conglomerates, ending up in the hands of Diageo who still own the rights.

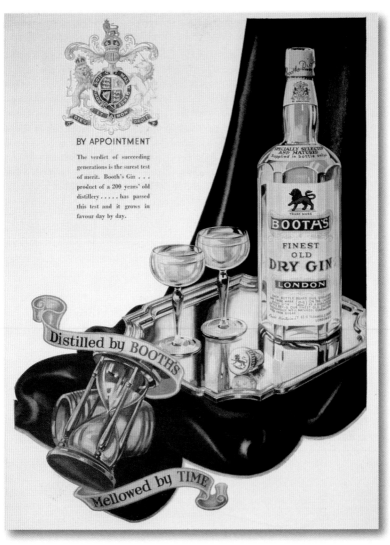

BY APPOINTMENT

The verdict of succeeding generations is the surest test of merit. Booth's Gin . . . product of a 200 years' old distillery . . . . . has passed this test and it grows in favour day by day.

Distilled by BOOTH'S

Mellowed by TIME

ABOVE: *The Royal seal of approval was a great selling point for Booth's Finest Old Dry Gin.*

BOUDIER SAFFRON GIN

Saffron Gin, made by Gabriel Boudier of Dijon, is a direct link to the gin-distilling history of northern France, which, as a former part of the Low Countries, was once a genever hub. Based on an old colonial recipe, Saffron Gin is rich in the exotic botanicals that were the fashion at that time – iris, fennel and of course, saffron. Saffron imparts a rich orange colour whilst a distinctive spiciness comes from fennel and angelica seed. Think of it as an alternative to Aperol, the Italian liqueur that has gained enormously in popularity of late, and serve either with tonic and a slice of orange or topped up with Cava or Prosecco for a perfect aperitif.

Orange slice, saffron and tonic

SAFFRON GIN *by* GABRIEL BOUDIER

BROKER'S GIN

Broker's Gin makes much of its English heritage with its bowler hat and city gent pinstripe packaging. It's distilled in a copper pot still at the Langley Distillery near Birmingham. The botanical mix, which includes cassia bark, cinnamon, liquorice and nutmeg, is steeped in neutral grain spirit made from 100% English wheat before distilling. The result is a very London-style gin with a rich aromatic nose. Spirits guru F. Paul Pacult summed up the taste experience: "In the mouth it sits well on the tongue and, thankfully, is the proper level of alcohol for gin, 94 proof (47% ABV). It finishes long, semi-sweet, tangy and luscious. A superbly made London Dry Gin that deserves a very close look by any admirer of that style."

BULLDOG GIN

Another very classic London Gin distilled in London and made from 100% British grain, Bulldog is triple-filtered for extra smoothness. Its makers have sought out the unusual and the exotic in terms of flavor, so botanicals include such eccentricities as lotus leaves, lavender, poppy and the reputedly aphrodisiac Dragon Eye, a cousin of the lychee fruit. Big, intense flavours, a good solid 40% ABV strength and lots of aromatic spice make this one for a Martini – especially the Dirty version with olive juice.

BURNETT'S WHITE SATIN

Burnett's White Satin is a venerable English brand that was established by Robert Burnett in the late 18th century. He acquired a huge distillery in Vauxhall that had been built in 1767 by Sir Joseph Mawbey. It was then the biggest in London and contemporary reports record that there were seldom fewer than 2,000 hogs constantly grunting, and kept entirely on the grains. (A common practice of distillers at the time was to keep pigs and feed them on the waste from distilling – very eco.) Robert Burnett became Sheriff of London in 1794 and was knighted the following year.

Burnett's White Satin is another classic English brand that has had its ups and downs. For years, it was one of the biggest-selling gins in the UK but then it became a cheap compounded gin made with a molasses spirit and artificial flavourings. It has now, however, regained its place as a traditionally distilled proper London Dry Gin at 40% ABV. Pleasantly junipery with warm spicy flavours, it's an everyday gin that is a very good alternative to domestic Gordon's for those who still smart at the latter's reduction in alcoholic strength.

Cadenhead's Old Raj gin is technically neither a London nor a Distilled Gin and is made by cold compounding. So why is it included here, you might ask? Because, despite this, it's a very good gin, most likely because it uses natural, not artificial flavourings and it has an exceptionally high alcoholic strength. It's made by macerating each botanical in a mixture of alcohol and water, then distilling them separately in a small pot still. The resulting infusions are combined with a neutral grain spirit and saffron is added for colouring. At 46% ABV, it is spirity and peppery with a slight medicinal taste, at 55% ABV it is very aromatic and rounded.

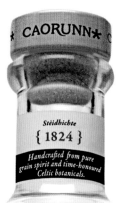

CAORUNN GIN

Scottish whisky distillers have been at the forefront of the great gin revival. It's not surprising – they have the stills, the spirit and generations of distilling expertise. Caorunn (pronounced "ka-roon") Gin is small batch gin made in Scotland by Inver House Distillers, the malt whisky experts who own Balmenach Distillery on Speyside.

Caorunn is Gaelic for the rowanberry and the gin includes rowanberries and a further 10 botanicals including some unusual, particularly Scottish ingredients – such as Coul Blush apple, heather, bog myrtle and dandelion – that grow in or near the distillery itself. It is made by a unique vapour infusion method whereby neutral grain spirit is heated to vapour in a special still called a copper berry chamber, made in the 1920s. The chamber is round and contains four large trays on which the botanicals are placed. As the vapour passes through the trays it picks up the flavours of the botanicals in a long slow process. When it cools and returns to liquid the botanicals are firmly embedded in the spirit.

Reduced to a bottling strength of 41.8% ABV, Caorunn is a real taste experience. On the nose it's juniper with fruity notes of rowan and apple that develop into a clean, crisp, aromatic flavour with a pronounced fruitiness and slight heather honey sweetness. A long dry finish makes this one for those who are fans of mellow gins. Try it in a Summer Gin Punch or as its signature serve with tonic water and a slice of red apple for garnish.

CITADELLE GIN

Another French gin, Citadelle is made in Ars by renowned distillers Gabriel & Andreu. It's based on an original 18th-century recipe from the former Citadelle Distillery in Dunkirk and is typical of French gins in that it is highly flavoursome and aromatic with rare botanicals such as savory, fennel, violets and star anise. Bottled at 44% ABV, the use of so many botanicals can somewhat overpower its juniper character but unusual herbal notes and a pleasantly perfumed palate more than make up for this.

CITY OF LONDON DRY GIN

City of London Dry Gin (or COLD Gin) is distilled at the City of London Distillery, which is the first distillery to be commissioned in the City of London for over 200 years. Bottled at 40% ABV, it's another super citrus gin with orange, lemon and grapefruit in the mix. This translates nicely into an almost lavender-like softness with heaps of zesty, almost sharp notes. This is a great gin for a Collins – either the traditional Tom or any one of the newer-style fruit Collinses that are so easy to make.

CORK DRY GIN

Cork Dry Gin was first made at the Old Watercourse Distillery near Cork in 1793, using spices and herbs brought to the port of Cork, then a great centre of trade. It's now owned by Pernod Ricard and made at the Midleton Distilleries in County Cork. Although it's not rated by knowledgeable gin-drinkers because it is a cold compounded gin, there is something very mellow and Irish about its sherbety, soft citrus flavours. It is bottled at 38% ABV but far better at its export strength of 43% ABV. It is the biggest-selling gin in Ireland.

DARNLEY'S VIEW GIN

When the Wemyss family, renowned for their expertise in fine wines and spirits, were thinking of a name for their new gin they naturally thought of their historic family home Wemyss Castle in Scotland – the place where Mary Queen of Scots first spied her future husband, Lord Darnley, in 1565. Bottled at 40% ABV, Darnley's View contains elderflower, nicely balanced by a hefty dose of juniper. Darnley's View is the ideal summer gin and works very well in summery drinks like the Elderflower Collins and the Gin Fizz.

In 2012 Darnley's View Spiced Gin was launched. It contains cinnamon, nutmeg, cassia, Grains of Paradise, ginger, cumin and cloves. These warm winter flavours go perfectly with Bitter Lemon, a mixer that we should see much more of nowadays.

DEATH'S DOOR GIN

US-based Death's Door Spirits work with local farmers in Wisconsin to grow organic and sustainable grains and have become a leading force in craft distilling. Bottled at 47% ABV, Death's Door Gin is made from a mix of local organic hard red winter wheat and organic malted barley. Unusually, they distil the base spirit themselves at their small craft distillery and it is then re-distilled with three botanicals – juniper, coriander and fennel. Not surprisingly given this minimalist approach, juniper dominates, enhanced by the green notes of celery and coriander.

DH KRAHN GIN

This US gin sits firmly in the London style in terms of taste, but is not produced like traditional London Gins. It is made by macerating botanicals and then re-distilling them with neutral spirit in a Stupfler pot still. The gin is then left to age slightly in steel barrels but no colour is picked up. The recipe is simple, with only six botanicals, and the addition of Thai ginger is inspired, adding an almost chilli tang to the sweet fruit and citrus profile. Ideal in a Martini.

DODD'S GIN

Dodd's Gin is made at the London Distillery in Battersea and named after Ralph Dodd, who first raised capital to set up the London Distillery Company in the 1800s. Neutral spirit is infused with eight botanicals that include the unusual fresh lime peel, bay laurel, two types of cardamom, red raspberry leaf and honey from the nearby London Honey Company. On tasting there's spicy warmth from the cardamom with citrus and a pleasant viscosity, possibly from the use of the honey.

EDINBURGH GIN

Edinburgh Gin is a small-batch, juniper-led gin with a Scottish twist. It starts life south of the Border at the Langley Distillery where Scottish grain spirit is distilled together with the classic gin botanicals in the traditional way. It is then shipped to Scotland where distinctively Scottish botanicals, in the form of less pungent Scottish juniper as well as heather and milk thistle, are added. Finally it is bottled at a hefty 43% ABV.

On the nose it's clean, fresh and spicy. In the mouth pine comes to the forefront with heathery scented notes following on. A well-balanced crisp gin with a gingery spiciness and laid-back citrus.

FIFTY POUNDS

Crafted at Thames Distillers in London, Fifty Pounds Gin takes its name from the unsuccessful 1736 Gin Act when a £50 tax was levied on those wishing to produce and sell gin. Only two distilleries ever agreed to pay it!

It has 11 botanicals including eight of the classics, but the remaining three are a secret. The spirit is rested for three weeks after distillation to allow the flavour of the botanicals to marry. Bottled at 43.5% ABV, Fifty Pounds Gin's intense clean flavours have made it a hit with gin-loving barkeeps all over the world. On the nose there's massive juniper, lemon zest and sage aromas. On tasting there's a bit of sweetness and a juniper, orange and lemon citrus-led palate with fresh minty notes emerging in the finish.

FORDS GIN

Distilled in London at Thames Distillers, Fords Gin is a collaboration between eighth-generation Master Distiller Charles Maxwell and Simon Ford of the 86 Co.

It has a mix of nine botanicals including three different types of citrus, extra floral in the form of jasmine flower and extra spice in the form of cassia. The botanicals are steeped for 15 hours before distillation in 500-litre copper stills.

Fords Gin has been created with the classic gin drinks in mind. At a hefty 45% ABV it has the firepower to make its presence felt in all types of cocktails, whilst its elegant citrus notes make it a delightful everyday drinking gin.

FOXDENTON ESTATE 48 GIN

Foxdenton 48 is made at Thames Distillers in London for Nicholas Radclyffe, the sixth generation of his family to own the Foxdenton estate in Buckinghamshire. It's a classic London Dry that has been developed specifically for the G and T.

A simple recipe with six botanicals, its point of difference is the use of lime flower oil to add subtle citrus notes. Big juniper combined with a refreshing citrus kick delivers everything one would expect from a classic English gin. The Foxdenton Company also makes a range of excellent fruit gins — sloe, raspberry, plum, blackcurrant and damson.

Walter and Alfred Gilbey were the sons of a Bishops Stortford coach operator. Returning to London in 1857 from active duty in the Crimean War, the two brothers set up a wine business in Soho importing fine wines from the colonies to cater to the needs of the new, prosperous middle class. By 1867 they had done so well that they were able to move their premises to the famous Pantheon building in Oxford Street. At about the same time, realizing that gin was becoming middle-class too, they started producing gin at their Camden Town distillery (now a block of chic apartments).

Success was rapid and, by the 1920s, Gilbey's had gin distilleries in Australia and Canada. During Prohibition the Gilbey's empire flourished and the Pantheon offices regularly dispatched consignments of gin for shipment to Antwerp and Hamburg. From there they were shipped to just outside the 12-mile limit and then into the States for customers who paid cash.

So popular was Gilbey's gin during Prohibition that it was widely counterfeited. To prevent this, special frosted bottles were introduced; only in 1975 did the company revert to the original clear glass style. By this time Gilbey's had distilleries in New Zealand, Uruguay, Namibia, East Africa, Swaziland, Mauritius and Mozambique.

The Gilbey's brand is now owned by Diageo and is rarely seen on UK shelves. It is still produced under licence in the United States, however, by Jim Beam Brands, as well as in Australia, Canada, New Zealand and South Africa, and remains a huge brand in Commonwealth countries.

GIN MARE

Produced in a fishing village on Spain's Costa Dorada, Gin Mare bills itself as the gin of the Mediterranean. Here traditional botanicals are enhanced by the more unusual olives, basil, rosemary and thyme. Production is unconventional too, with all the botanicals save the citrus ones macerated individually in neutral grain alcohol, and then distilled in a copper pot still, again individually. Then all the botanicals are blended together and bottled at 42.7% ABV.

The result is very different from English-style gin: more like a juniper-flavoured schnapps with interesting herbal, savoury notes enhanced by the pungency of rosemary.

GORDON'S SPECIAL DRY GIN

Alexander Gordon was born in London on 10 August 1742. His father, George Gordon, was a native of Aberdeen, who allegedly left Scotland due to his involvement in the 1715 Jacobite uprising. Alexander founded his distilling business in Southwark, in 1769, and then moved it, in 1786, to Clerkenwell. He had 10 children, one of whom, Charles, carried on the

MEDITERRANEAN GIN
Colección de autor.

GIN MARE

DISTILLED FROM OLIVES, THYME, ROSEMARY AND BASIL.

700 ml. Alc. 42,7 % vol.

family business when Alexander died. His son, another Charles, sold the firm in 1878 to John Currie & Co.

Distillers at the Four Mills Distillery at Bromley by Bow, Currie & Co had provided Gordon's with spirit for rectification for many years. Tanqueray already had a close commercial relationship with Currie's and, in 1898, Gordon and Tanqueray combined to create Tanqueray, Gordon & Co. This move established the two companies as the most powerful force in English distilling, a position they still hold in the firm embrace of distilling giant Diageo.

Gordon's today is the global number-two-selling gin. Its UK base is Cameronbridge in Scotland but it also produces gin in the United States, Canada, South America and Jamaica.

Gordon's is a very traditional London Gin made to the original recipe which specifies ginger, cassia oil and nutmeg as well as the more commonly found juniper and coriander. Sold in the UK at 37.5% ABV, it is very juniper and lemon sherbety in a way that works well in a Gin and Tonic, which is how it's mostly drunk. Gordon's Export Strength at 47.3% ABV is a totally different experience – it's available in the UK as Gordon's Yellow Label and in worldwide duty-free and it's always worth seeking out. Gordon's has also launched new cucumber and elderflower-flavoured gins.

GREENALL'S ORIGINAL LONDON DRY

G & J Greenall has been producing gin since 1761, the year that Thomas Dakin built a distillery in the centre of Warrington, then a great centre for brewing and distilling. In 1870, Edward Greenall, a member of an established Lancashire brewing family, bought the Dakin company and acquired ownership of a successful business with an established distribution network.

In the mid-1960s, a new distillery, bottling facilities and warehouses were built on land close to the site of the original distillery. Disaster struck in 2005, when the entire premises were almost destroyed by fire. But the distillery was saved and was able to continue to make a number of prestigious gins. In fact Greenall's are the second-largest gin distiller in the UK, making many very good supermarket own-label gins.

Greenall's Original contains eight different botanicals, including the less common cassia bark and ground almonds. Bottled at 40% ABV, it's strongly citrus on the nose, developing into dry rounded juniper notes. The company also makes a range of Gin and Tonic in cans with huge markets in Eastern Europe, particularly in Russia, where people are regularly spotted downing them on the way to work in the morning.

G'VINE

G'Vine gins are the brainchild of EuroWineGate, the French company who make Ciroc, the first vodka made

from grapes, not grain or potatoes. They've extended the neutral wine spirit theory into gin production and G'Vine is made from Ugni Blanc grapes. The signature flavour of G'Vine Floraison is the rare vine flower, which blooms for a few days in June (this blossoming period is known in France as the floraison, hence the name). It is combined with other botanicals such as ginger root, liquorice, green cardamom, cassia bark, cubeb berries, nutmeg and lime. G'Vine Nouaison, named for the berry on the vine, has increased juniper and nutmeg, less vine flower and is bottled at a higher 43.9% ABV.

Whilst G'Vine gins may not be for the juniper purist, their light, floaty, floral flavours come to the fore in citrus-based drinks, especially when lime is in the mix.

HAYMAN'S GINS

The Haymans are one of the oldest English distilling families still involved in the trade and the current Chairman, Christopher, is the great-grandson of James Burrough who created Beefeater Gin in the 1800s. (The other even older gin family is that of Charles Maxwell, Master Distiller at Thames Distillers, whose gincestry goes back to the 1700s.) Rather like their illustrious ancestor, Hayman's Distillers make several different types of gin. Hayman's London Dry Gin is a fine example of the classic handcrafted London style. The mix of 10 botanicals is steeped with triple-distilled neutral grain spirit in a traditional pot still for 24 hours before distilling begins. The result is a crisp and elegant gin in which juniper, coriander and strong citrus elements are carefully balanced.

The company has also led the revival of Old Tom gin. Hayman's Old Tom is distilled

from an original family recipe from the 1870s with more pungent botanicals like nutmeg, cassia bark, cinnamon and liquorice, and sweetened with sugar. It's an authentic re-creation of the Old Tom style once made by most English distillers, with one crucial difference: the spirit is properly rectified. It's much sought after by bartenders who want to experiment with original cocktail recipes from the glory days.

Hayman's 1820 Gin Liqueur is similar to the cordial gins of bygone days. It's made from 100% pure grain spirit and a subtle blend of botanicals with aromatic juniper and fruity notes. It should be drunk neat as a *digestif*.

HENDRICK'S GIN

Some years ago, when whisky experts William Grant & Sons decided to create a new gin, their inspiration was the traditional flavours of English summer. For months, the team worked in the lab, endlessly experimenting with different botanicals in the quest to get the right balance. After much trial and error, they arrived at the final botanicals – juniper, orris root, angelica, coriander, lemon and orange peel, caraway seeds, chamomile flowers, elderflowers, cubeb berries and meadowsweet with a final infusion of distilled oils

of cucumber and Bulgarian *rosa damascena* (Damascus rose).

Having developed an unusual recipe, it's not surprising that William Grant should adopt a different approach to making their new baby. Hendrick's is small-batch distilled using two different methods – pot still and infusion. The two distillates are then combined and cucumber and rose distillates added.

The percentage of pot-distilled to infusion-distilled is part of its secret recipe. But the combination of strong, aromatic flavours achieved in a pot still with the more subtle, volatile flavours picked up in the Carterhead is obvious in the final taste of Hendrick's.

It results in fresh, floral, slightly aromatic notes, combined with silky smooth texture and mouthfeel. Hendrick's is one of the prime movers in gin's glorious renaissance as its lighter, more floral taste profile has opened up a raft of new drinking possibilities – not just the famous Hendrick's serve of a Gin and Tonic with a wedge of cucumber, but delicious summery drinks like the elderflower Martini as well.

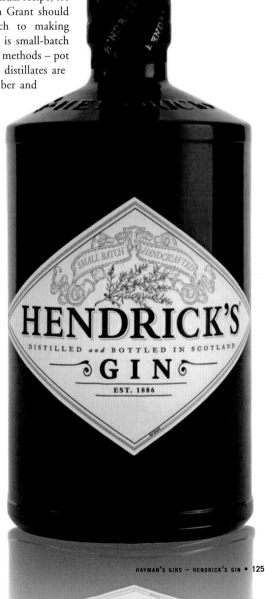

JENSEN'S BERMONDSEY GIN

Jensen's Bermondsey Gin is the brainchild of Christian Jensen, a Danish IT specialist who apparently fell in love with old-style gins while working in Japan and went on to develop his own gin. Since he is based in Bermondsey, he named the result Jensen's London-Distilled Dry Bermondsey Gin.

The emphasis here is on juniper-led flavours that are derived from a small number of ingredients used in traditional London Dry Gins. Bottled at 43% ABV, Jensen's is a taste of the past and rumour has it that it is a re-creation of a once very famous brand – Nicholson's Lamplighter Gin. Its heavier, more aromatic style makes it a good choice for many of the classic gin drinks from the golden age of cocktails. Jensen's also make an Old Tom gin.

JUNIPER GREEN ORGANIC GIN

The world's first gin certified organic by the Soil Association, Juniper Green is distilled at the Thames Distillery in London. Juniper Green is a proper London Dry Gin. A simple recipe of organic juniper, coriander, angelica and savory is combined with an exceptionally clean spirit distilled from organic grain. And for those who are wheat-intolerant the extra good news is that it's 100% gluten-free.

On the palate Juniper Green is light and elegant, with a gentle burst of spice and strong juniper. Although it's annoying that the producers have chosen to follow Gordon's down the route of a 37.5% ABV, Juniper Green is constantly raved about in blind tastings and the lower alcoholic strength is reflected in competitive pricing. A stalwart everyday gin.

JUNIPERO GIN

Made by Anchor Distilling, who started the craft beer movement in the US, Junipero Gin is produced at a small distillery in San Francisco. It is a classic Dry style of gin made with 12 botanicals in a small copper pot still. Its makers are coy about the exact ingredients, but tasting reveals strong juniper, liquorice and grapefruit as well as other citrus. At 49.3% ABV, it's a big complex gin with a pronounced spiciness.

LARIOS GIN

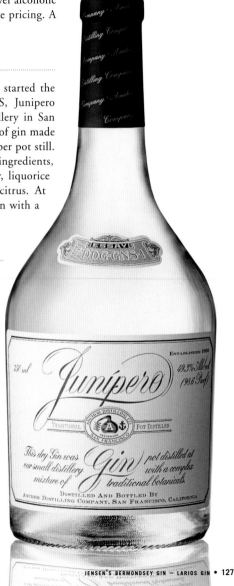

Spain is a gin-lover's paradise, with the *Gin Tonica* the drink of choice – and what a choice, with literally hundreds of brands and different types of tonic water to experiment with. The only true locally made international brand is Larios, a gin that is very much in the London Dry style, ie double-distilled, aromatic and unsweetened with strong juniper flavours evident. Bottled at 40% ABV, it is drunk in vast quantities often in the famous Gin Larios con Coca-Cola, which is really rather good.

A premium expression, Larios 12, named after its 12 botanicals,

contains nutmeg, angelica and masses of citrus in the form of lemon, orange, mandarin, tangerine, clementine, watermelon and lime. Here, the spirit and the botanicals are distilled together whilst a fifth distillation adds an infusion of orange blossom. Soft on the nose with hints of citrus developing into warm juniper and spice, try it with Coca-Cola but only the full-fat version, and make as you would a G and T.

LONDON HILL

Whisky experts Ian Macleod Distillers make London Hill Gin in the traditional way in copper pot stills. In addition to the four core botanicals, it also has cassia, ginger, nutmeg and liquorice, giving a nicely rounded profile with juniper dominant, just as it should be. London Hill gin consistently wins awards at spirit competitions judged by experts but it's not nearly as widely recognized as it deserves to be.

MAGELLAN GIN

This French gin is named after the famous 16th-century Portuguese explorer Ferdinand Magellan. After his death in the Philippines, his ship reputedly returned laden with cloves. So the signature botanical of this rather stylish gin is cloves, accompanied by cinnamon, cassia, nutmeg and Grains of Paradise alongside the conventional gin botanicals. It's made from triple-distilled French wheat that is re-distilled with the botanicals, and a final infusion of iris results in a deep blue colour.

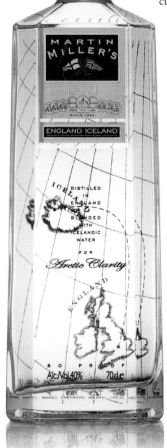

MARTIN MILLER'S GIN

The invention of the late Martin Miller, publisher of the famous *Miller's Antique Price Guides* and serial entrepreneur, Martin Miller's Gin is made at the Langley Distillery in a century-old gem of a copper pot still named "Angela". The botanicals recipe includes the less often used cassia and cinnamon bark, ground nutmeg and liquorice plus one other secret ingredient, almost certainly cucumber. Like all gins, Martin Miller's is reduced with demineralized water to its bottling strength of 40% ABV. This gin goes a bit further, taking the spirit on a 3,000-mile round trip to Iceland to be blended with what is considered to be the purest water on the planet. It may be this glacial water that makes Martin Miller's so exceptionally smooth and silky. What we end up with undoubtedly is a gentle gin with fragrant, slightly spicy aromas and strong hints of Parma violet and lavender. This unique taste profile makes Martin Miller's ideal in new-style cocktails like the Bramble.

MARTIN MILLER'S WESTBOURNE STRENGTH

Named after Martin Miller's original base in west London, Martin Miller's Westbourne Strength Gin is made identically to its sister brand but parts company in that it is bottled at the much higher 45.2% ABV. It's interesting to compare how much of a difference raising the alcoholic strength of a gin can make even when it's the same recipe. At 45.2% Westbourne Strength veers towards the more classic London flavour with lots of juniper, spice and citrus flavours.

MONKEY 47 GIN

Made by Black Forest Distillers in, yes, Germany's Black Forest (*Schwarzwald*), Monkey 47 is named for its alcoholic strength and the number of botanicals used in its recipe. The 47 include rarities such as spruce tips, cranberries, sage and verbena, many of which are handpicked in the Black Forest itself.

On tasting, the base spirit appears more aromatic and less "neutral" than the grain spirit used in British gins, but that could also be explained by the diversity of the botanical flavourings. Aromatic and herbal, Monkey 47 is reminiscent of old-style gins that had a stronger connection to Dutch genever. Which makes it the perfect gin to experiment with in original golden age cocktails – especially ones with vermouth and/ or bitters.

NO. 3 ST. JAMES LONDON DRY GIN

When the renowned wine and spirits merchants Berry Bros & Rudd create a gin, one can be confident it will be top-quality. No. 3 Gin is named for the company's famous shop in St James Street in the heart of London, founded in 1698 by the Widow Bourne. That original shop is still the oldest wine and spirit merchant in the UK and a Mecca for lovers of fine drink.

It still has the original scales that were also used to weigh the shop's many notable customers, such as Lord Byron, Horatio Nelson, Lady Hamilton and William Pitt.

Made in Schiedam, Holland's distilling centre and gin's ancestral home, No. 3 is the Platonic ideal of a classic London Dry Gin bottled at a serious 46% ABV. The botanical mix of juniper, coriander, sweet orange peel, angelica, grapefruit peel and cardamom is left to steep overnight before distillation in traditional copper pot stills. On the nose there's a welcome blast of piney juniper with citrus and coriander very evident. In the mouth the juniper develops into a crispness nicely balanced by gentle cardamom spiciness. Perfect for a Dry Martini and a Negroni where one wants big, bold flavours.

NO. 209 GIN

No. 209 Gin is made in San Francisco in a specially commissioned Scottish copper pot still based on the design of the Glenmorangie

whisky stills, which were in fact originally used for making gin. It's a robust gin, built around the signature botanicals of bergamot, sweet orange, cardamom and cassia as well as the more usual juniper and citrus. On the palate are pleasant lavender and floral notes that combine well with the bittersweet juniper. It's a favourite of bartenders who recommend No. 209 in a Gin Mojito.

OPIHR GIN

A spiced gin, Opihr Oriental Gin references the fabled port of Biblical times and the centuries-old spice route from the Far East. Made in the more prosaic surrounding of Warrington by Quintessential, it has been developed by Master Distiller Joanne Moore, one of the UK's two female head distillers. Lots of spice – cubebs from Indonesia, cumin from Turkey, and cardamom, ginger and black pepper from India, combine to produce aromatic and warming flavours. Spice and juniper are perfectly balanced and coriander also comes through strongly. Works well when mixed with the extra spice of ginger beer and also in a punch.

OXLEY CLASSIC ENGLISH GIN

Bacardi-owned Oxley Spirits Company spent eight years developing Oxley Gin and, along the way, introduced a whole new way of distilling gin. In a major technological advance, it is the first-ever spirit created by cold distillation. So instead of heat being applied to reduce the spirit and botanicals to vapour, vacuum is used to reduce the pressure in the still and lower the temperature to approximately −5° C. At this temperature the spirit, which has been macerated for 15 hours, becomes vapour. It then meets a cold finger probe (chilled to −100° C) and reverts back to liquid to be collected for bottling.

The bespoke still at London's Thames Distillers produces only 120 bottles per batch and a major advantage of cold distillation is that there are no heads or tails – so less wastage than traditional distillation methods. But all that would be meaningless without some real impact on flavour. And here Oxley delivers big-time. The 14 botanicals include the traditional ones as well as three different types of fresh citrus – grapefruit, orange and lemon – and exotics like vanilla and meadowsweet. It's slightly spicy on the nose with hints of lavender, almond, marshmallow and soft citrus; juniper is evident but not dominant. Think soft and scented rather than oily and pungent. What stands out, however, are the exceptionally clean and fresh flavours and the texture and purity of the spirit that is holding these complex aromas together. At 47% ABV Oxley is an intense, flavourful gin and it's one of the few gins that can happily be drunk neat over ice in a balloon glass, ideally with a grapefruit twist.

PICKERING'S GIN

Pickering's Gin is a prime example of the craft distilling movement that is sweeping the UK. Made in Edinburgh by two self-confessed gin nuts at the arts complex Summerhall, formerly the University's Veterinary School aka the Dick Vet, it's based on an old colonial recipe handed down to founder Marcus Pickering's family. Pickering and partner Matt Gammell have transformed what were once the vet school's dog kennels into a small but perfectly formed distillery complete with bespoke copper pot still. Cleverly they've also run a line into Summerhall's bar, The Royal Dick, so that Pickering is available there on tap.

Bottled at 42% ABV, the recipe has nine botanicals including cardamom, fennel, anise, lemon, lime and cloves. Astonishingly for gin novices, they have actually invented a "bain marie" system to provide a more consistent heat to the still. Very small-batch, Pickering's is strongly aromatic in the mouth with hints of liquorice and cinnamon, slightly nutty notes, fresh citrus and a lavender-like softness. The distillery will also be open to the public – see *Gin Places* on page 187.

Plymouth Gin has a long history and dates back to at least 1793 when a young Mr Coates joined distillers based at the Black Friars building in Southside Street, Plymouth. The mediaeval Black Friars is also indisputably the oldest working distillery in the country. A deed of sale dated 12 November 1697 refers to a "mault-house" on the premises and it is clear that Black Friars was used for making alcohol from the birth of legal commercial distilling in England. When distilling was deregulated in 1690, malting grain, brewing, distilling and rectifying (the process of re-distilling spirit to make gin) were complementary activities, often carried out under the same roof. Only in 1825 did it become illegal to produce the base spirit and re-distilled gin at the same location. Descriptions of Black Friars after that date refer only to a distillery so, obviously, Messrs Coates' business was now successful enough to focus exclusively on making gin and other "rectified" spirits.

There is a great misconception that Plymouth is a different "style" of gin. It isn't, it's made in exactly the same way as a London Dry but it does not carry the London Dry label. In fact it was the only UK gin to have a geographic indication – a bit like an *appellation contrôlée*. This does not relate to its production methods but is the result of a series of legal verdicts in the 1880s when a London distiller began producing a "Plymouth" gin. Owners Coates & Co won several suits under the "passing off" legislation, establishing that Plymouth Gin could only be made within Plymouth city walls, by law. The GI status has been dropped but the unique nature of Plymouth Gin stays the same.

Produced in a still that has stood for over 150 years, Plymouth Gin has a subtle, full-bodied flavour with no bitter botanicals. A higher than usual proportion of root ingredients is the source of Plymouth's distinctive, earthy, rooty tastes, whilst the additions of sweet orange and cardamom impart a softly fruity, spicy finish. Pure water from Dartmoor contributes to its exceptionally clean and fresh flavour.

The gin of the Royal Navy, the gin of the world's first Martini recipe, Sir Winston Churchill's favourite gin and once the biggest-selling English gin brand in the world, Plymouth Gin fell on hard times in the 1970s. But it's now firmly back, ensconced as a sister brand to Beefeater and Beefeater 24. Plymouth Original is bottled at 41.2% ABV whilst Plymouth Navy Strength comes in at a whopping 57% ABV. Plymouth also produces sloe gin and damson gin and has an excellent visitor centre where you can learn all you ever need to know about gin – see *Gin Places* on page 187.

PORTOBELLO ROAD NO. 171 GIN

BELOW: *This sign is inside the bar at No. 171 Portobello Road in west London. As well as the bar, there is a working distillery and a museum (the Ginstitute) on the premises.*

Above the Portobello Star bar along London's famous Portobello Road is the Ginstitute, the smallest gin museum in London, the home of gin. Most importantly it also contains the city's smallest working copper pot still – "Coppernicus". Owners Ged Feltham and Jake Burger devised their gin recipe here and it is now commercially produced at nearby Thames Distillers in Clapham.

Portobello Road No. 171 uses nine botanicals, majoring on warm spice botanicals like cassia bark, liquorice and nutmeg. Citrus in the form of lemon and bitter orange comes through strongly and somehow, although there is neither cardamom nor grapefruit in the recipe, one picks up hints of aromatic cardamom and grapefruit on the nose. At 42% ABV, Portobello comes into its own in tonic water where robustness is required. See *Gin Places* on page 187 for further information on the Ginstitute.

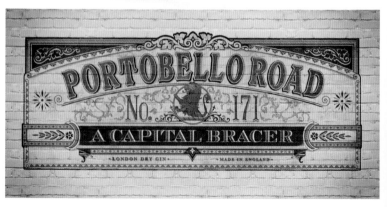

SACRED GIN

The Sacred Distillery in London's Highgate is actually located in founder Ian Hart's back garden, so it could not be more micro. The gin is made with 12 botanicals including lemon and lime, cardamom, nutmeg, and a very unusual botanical, Boswellia Sacra (aka frankincense) from which the product derives its name.

The distillation process is unusual too as, instead of a traditional copper pot still, Sacred is made under low pressure vacuum. Each of the 12 botanicals is distilled separately using English grain spirit and then blended to make the final spirit, which is bottled at 40% ABV. The idea here is the that separate, low-pressure, low-temperature distillations are able to extract maximum flavour from each different botanical.

On tasting Sacred is lush and fruity with very big and clean flavours and slightly scented notes derived from the frankincense. It works well with cranberry juice and bitter lemon. The company also produce a Gin Blending Kit that allows gin-lovers to blend their own gin as well as a very delicious gin-based Rosehip Cup.

SEAGRAM'S GINS

Seagram's Extra Dry is the US equivalent of Gordon's in the UK – a huge-volume brand that outsells its nearest competitors by a country mile. For that reason, it is not appreciated as much as it really ought to be. Known as "the

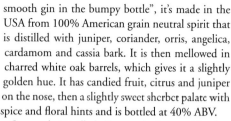

smooth gin in the bumpy bottle", it's made in the USA from 100% American grain neutral spirit that is distilled with juniper, coriander, orris, angelica, cardamom and cassia bark. It is then mellowed in charred white oak barrels, which gives it a slightly golden hue. It has candied fruit, citrus and juniper on the nose, then a slightly sweet sherbet palate with spice and floral hints and is bottled at 40% ABV.

Seagram's Distiller's Reserve is the combination of the best of the barrels as selected by the Master Distiller. The higher strength of the spirit at 51% ABV is definitely noticeable when it is sipped straight.

SIPSMITH LONDON DRY GIN

Sipsmith London Dry Gin is produced in Chiswick in three bespoke copper pot stills – Prudence, Patience and Constance. The spirit is made by hand in genuinely small batches, never more than 500 bottles a time, often considerably less, by Master Distiller Jared Brown who is also a well-known cocktail historian. The botanicals include the familiar ones as well as liquorice, ground almonds, cassia bark and cinnamon, making it very much a classic London Dry Gin. The aromas are of citrus with a meadow-like herbaceousness, whilst on the palate it opens up to distinctive juniper, sweet orange and lemon marmalade.

This makes it an ideal spirit for a Gin and Tonic or Gin Collins. The Sipsmith range also includes a sloe gin, barley vodka and Summer Cup – a new take on a Pimm's-style drink – plus VJOP, very junipery over proof gin, a wow at 57.5% ABV.

SIX O'CLOCK GIN

Produced by Bramley and Gage who are known for their excellent fruit liqueurs, the essence of the English countryside, Six O'Clock Gin is a breath of fresh air. It's made from seven botanicals including elderflower and savory and is bottled at a respectable 43% ABV. Exceptionally clean and fresh in the mouth, it combines the traditional juniper character of gin with graceful floral notes. Cleverly Bramley and Gage have launched a tonic water to accompany it. Six O'Clock Tonic is all natural with no saccharin or sodium benzoate. Instead natural quinine extracts with infusions of lemon and lime create a clean-tasting, not over-sweet mixer that is designed to enhance its sister gin.

SLOANE'S GIN

Sloane's Gin is named after Sir Hans Sloane (1660–1753), a Royal Physician, botanist, collector, lifelong benefactor and landlord of the Physic Garden Chelsea (close to Sloane Square – also named for him).

Made by blending 10 separately distilled botanical distillates, Sloane's Gin combines flavours from across the botanical spectrum – citrus, spice, juniper, floral from the use of iris root and a musky sweetness from vanilla. The gin is left to settle for a month to allow the different flavours to marry together. At 40% ABV the result is a soft, well-balanced gin that goes down smoothly and works well in a range of mixed drinks and cocktails.

ORIGINAL

Premium Dry

SLOANE'S

DISTILLED
GIN

ORIGINAL

40%vol 70cl

Coriander Seeds

Juniper Berries

Vanilla Pods

INDIVIDUALLY DISTILLED

Sloanes Gin is made in small batches and unlike other gins, each botanical is distilled individually having been steeped in liquor for 24 hours. After the distillation there is a further period of rest for a minimum of one month. The distiller is then able to marry the distilled botanicals to make the perfect premium gin.

SW4 GIN

SW4 Gin embodies the desire of owner Martin Price to produce a proper old-style London Dry Gin that wouldn't be overpowered by strongly flavoured mixers.

There are 12 botanicals in the SW4 Gin, the standards plus nutmeg, savory, liquorice, cassia, almond and both orange and lemon peel. The mix is steeped for approximately 12 hours in grain spirit before being distilled in small batches. Two strengths of SW4 Gin are available – a standard 40% ABV and a much stronger version at 47% ABV. In the 40% ABV SW4 Gin there is an initial juniper hit followed by citrus and spice with the citrus contributing orange marmalade and lemon curd flavours. As with most classic London Dry Gins there's a long clean finish with dryness very obvious in the back of the mouth. This is a perfect gin for new-style lemonades such as those as produced by Fentimans.

TANQUERAY

Charles Tanqueray, born in 1810, was the descendant of Huguenots and came from a long line of clergymen. The distilling business of Edward & Charles Tanqueray & Co, Rectifiers, was established by 1838 on Vine Street at the southern edge of Bloomsbury. However, according to a property deed of the same year, the site had been used as a distillery for some time.

In his Bloomsbury Distillery, Charles Tanqueray wanted to produce a quality gin, and after years of experimentation, he finally produced his unique recipe.

Tanqueray Gin met with instant success and a prestigious clientele. Soon,

Tanqueray stoneware crocks, used in the trade until 1900, were to be seen in the better class of grocer and wine and spirit merchants as well as in discerning households. (He did not deal in bulk-casked gin for ordinary taverns.) Within a few years, Tanqueray Gin was being exported to the British colonies while still much in demand at home.

Tanqueray and Gordon's joined forces in 1898. In the 1950s the decision was taken to focus Tanqueray on the export market, particularly the US where it was the favourite tipple of celebrities such as Bob Hope, Frank Sinatra and Sammy Davis Junior. Frustratingly this meant that for many years Tanqueray was barely available in the UK, but one of the benefits of the great gin revival has been the relaunch of Tanqueray on its home turf.

Today, the Tanqueray name is found on three quite different gins ...

TANQUERAY RANGPUR

The newest addition to the Tanqueray family, Tanqueray Rangpur is made with fresh Rangpur limes, juniper and bay leaf. It falls between a traditional Dry and a fruit gin with a distinctive lime taste. Mix with cranberry juice for a Rangpur Cran or with ginger ale and a few drops of bitters for a Rangpur Ginger.

All Tanqueray gins are exclusively made in the UK at Diageo's distilleries in Cameronbridge, Scotland.

TANQUERAY SPECIAL DRY GIN

Tanqueray Special Dry Gin is a London Dry with knobs on, greeting one boisterously with a lovely juniper-fresh welcome. Although the recipe is still secret, Special Dry is believed to contain only four botanicals, proof that sometimes less is more and that the balance of ingredients is key to taste. On tasting, juniper and liquorice are very obvious as is a subtle spiciness most likely derived from coriander. At a high-strength 47% ABV, based on a clean grain spirit, it is exceptionally dry. There's also a 43.1% ABV version, which is just as good.

TANQUERAY 10

A radical addition to the gin category when it launched in 2000, Tanqueray 10 was created specifically for Martinis. Made in small batches in a swan neck still known as "Tiny Ten", it adds fresh citrus in the form of limes, oranges and grapefruit as well as chamomile to the botanical mix. The more volatile citrus is distilled first with pure grain spirit and then re-distilled with the traditional Tanqueray botanicals. Extra fresh citrus is added to the final spirit. Juniper is at the heart of this gin, but is relatively laid-back when compared to big gins like Tanqueray Special Dry. It's very citrusy, clean and as fresh as a meadow with soothing notes of chamomile.

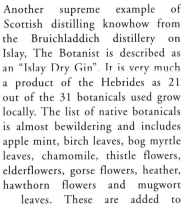

THE BOTANIST

Another supreme example of Scottish distilling knowhow from the Bruichladdich distillery on Islay, The Botanist is described as an "Islay Dry Gin". It is very much a product of the Hebrides as 21 out of the 31 botanicals used grow locally. The list of native botanicals is almost bewildering and includes apple mint, birch leaves, bog myrtle leaves, chamomile, thistle flowers, elderflowers, gorse flowers, heather, hawthorn flowers and mugwort leaves. These are added to more traditional gin botanicals and distilled in a low-pressure Lomond pot still. At 46% ABV The Botanist is an intense and very complex gin but retains a strong juniper character despite the number of botanical flavourings used. Clean, bone-dry with subtle floral and herbal flavours, it lends itself to Martinis and many of the new-style fruit-based Collinses.

CONCEIVED, DISTILLED & HAND-CRAFTED
ON THE ISLAND OF ISLAY

THE BOTANIST

ISLAY DRY GIN

22

FORAGED ISLAND BOTANICALS

TRIFOLIUM REPENS
CRATAEGUS MONOGYNA
MELISSA OFFICINALIS
THYMUS POLYTRICHUS
MENTHA X VILLOSA
BETULA PUBESCENS
FILIPENDULA ULMARIA

THE LONDON No 1

The London No 1 Gin is unusual in that it's blue, the colour being derived from an infusion of gardenia flowers. Its base is a spirit made from Suffolk and Norfolk grain re-distilled with 13 botanicals including liquorice root, savory, cinnamon and cassia bark. London No 1 Gin also features bergamot, that instantly recognizable perfumed aroma so familiar in Earl Grey tea. Rested for three weeks after distillation in a pot still, the result is a very English-style Distilled Gin. At a generous 47% ABV, The London Gin is elegant on the nose with marked spicy and balsamic notes. Soft, elegant and mellow in the mouth with a lingering spiciness, it's a sophisticated, well-rounded gin with slightly perfumed qualities that make it an ideal partner for cranberry juice.

WARNER EDWARDS GIN

Warner Edwards Harrington Gin is made in a barn on a farm in Northamptonshire using locally grown botanicals such as elderflower and lavender. Most of the water used for reduction is from a local spring. So it couldn't be more local and more in tune with the trend for proving provenance. At 44% ABV it has a spicy fragrant core with lots of mellow sweetness.

WHITLEY NEILL LONDON DRY

Whitley Neill is a premium London Dry Gin, created by Johnny Neill, the fourth generation of the Greenall Whitley distilling family. It's made from a 100% grain spirit that is steeped with the botanicals prior to distillation in antique copper pot stills. The recipe took some time to formulate as the producers were determined to bring something new to the party. The result is nine botanicals consisting of core botanicals and the addition of two signature elements from Africa – the Cape gooseberry and the fruit of the Baobab tree, the tree of life. The taste experience starts with a spicy freshness on the nose. Laid-back juniper and citrus combine with the fresh tanginess of the wild fruit to create robust yet delicate and clean flavours. A pleasant lingering finish holds those flavours in the mouth whilst an alcoholic strength of 42% ABV ensures perfect balance.

XORIGUER GIN DE MAHON

A bit of an oddity. Xoriguer Gin de Mahon is now the only gin with a geographic distinction: it can only be made in Mahon on the Balearic island of Menorca. Gin distilling there dates from the British presence in the 18th century when

Menorca was an important British naval base. British soldiers and sailors stationed in Mahon wanted gin, the fashionable spirit at home, so enterprising local distilleries started making it from juniper berries distilled with a spirit made from the local wine.

The Xoriguer distillery, founded and still owned by the Pons family, is now the only gin distillery on the island. There, Gin de Mahon is made, as it always has been, from a wine distillate in ancient copper stills heated by wood-burning fires. Once distilled, it is stored in large oak barrels and bottled at 40% ABV.

Only members of the Pons family know the exact ingredients of the Xoriguer recipe. It certainly has juniper and other aromatic herbs. Tasting reveals a brandy-like flavour with notes of caraway, fennel and orris. Xoriguer Gin is sold in green glass bottles with handles that copy old Dutch stone genever crocks. It is drunk widely on the island, particularly during the summer-long season of fiestas when it is mixed with lemonade in a drink called Pomada. It tastes innocuous but be warned, it packs a real punch – as the many British visitors to Menorca can attest.

ZUIDAM GIN

Given the ever-increasing popularity of London-style gin it's no wonder that Dutch distillers are reclaiming the distilling high ground and turning their attention to gin. There are quite a few brands of Dutch London Dry-style gin on the market but this high-strength 44.5% ABV Dry Gin from the family-owned Zuidam Distillers in Holland stands out. It contains nine botanicals – fresh sweet oranges and lemons, not the more conventional peels, whole bean vanilla, liquorice root and cardamom. The result is a big gin, strong in juniper but with a fiery sweetness.

AGED GINS

Of late there is a trend for ageing gin in wood, some say to re-create the gin of the 19th century when it was stored and transported in wooden barrels. The authenticity argument is not particularly convincing because the wood used to make storage barrels was very old wood that had been used many times and probably would not have imparted flavour. Secondly the implication that somehow the gin of the Victorian gin palace was inherently better than modern gin is just not realistic. In fact the opposite is true: modern distilling techniques and stricter quality controls mean that we now live in a golden age of gin production. That said, however, if the aim is purely to bring something new to the party in terms of flavour, aged gins certainly do the trick. They also expand our drinking repertoires to include gin as a *digestif* akin to a fine malt whisky or venerable old rum. Aged gins are usually fairly limited-edition bottlings, hence more likely to be available from specialist retailers, and include:

Burrough's Reserve: Created by Master Distiller Desmond Payne from an ancient recipe devised by founder James Burrough, the spirit is uniquely rested in Jean de Lillet oak barrels.

Citadelle Réserve: Aged for six months in oak, it has a fuller juniper taste with a slight oakiness and is bottled at 44% ABV.

Hayman's 1850 Reserve: Distilled to a recipe from 1850 and rested for three to four weeks in Scotch whisky barrels.

BANANA GIN

Banana gin is not a gin at all; it's the generic name for strong spirits in many parts of West Africa. This is a hangover from the shameful trading habits of the 18th century when the Dutch and English used genever and gin as a component of the "triangular trade". Their ships took goods – including spirits – to Africa, exchanged them for slaves which they transported to the Caribbean and the Americas, and there loaded up with sugar and tobacco which they brought back home. To this day original stone genever bottles are regularly dug up in remote parts of West Africa, a reminder of this practice. But today's banana "gins" are essentially fruit schnapps-type spirits usually made from bananas – hence the name. They are principally used for ritual purposes, for example poured out onto the ground as a ceremonial offering. Frankly this is the best thing to do with them.

DUTCH GENEVER

There are three styles of genever – oude, jonge and korenwijn – and there are aged and unaged varieties. Under European law, each style of genever must contain different minimum percentages of maltwine (a grain spirit with a fiery taste and a distinctive spirity character), botanicals and sugar, and be bottled at different alcoholic strengths. This is how it works:

OUDE GENEVER is the traditional genever, similar in taste to the original English Genevas. It must contain a minimum of 15% maltwine, no more than 20 grammes of sugar per litre and be bottled at at least 35% ABV. It does not have to be aged but often is. It also often has far higher percentages of maltwine than required.

JONGE GENEVER was developed in the 1950s in response to the demand for a more mixable, lighter-flavoured spirit. It is bottled at a minimum of 35% ABV and contains a maximum of 15% maltwine and no more than 10 grammes of sugar per litre. If the label mentions *graanjenever* [grain genever], then the base spirit is 100% grain. Jonge genever is colourless and very light on the palate.

The terms "oude" [old] and "jonge" [young] are confusing as one naturally thinks of aged and unaged. But in this case, they refer to "old style" and "new style".

KORENWIJN (or corenwyn) contains a minimum of 51% maltwine so it has a very malty, full-bodied taste. It must be at least 38% ABV and contain no more than 20 grammes of sugar per litre. Korenwijn is quite rare outside the Benelux countries but if you come across it, it's definitely worth a try. It's the Dutch equivalent of single-malt whisky. Drink it ice-cold on its own, or try it mixed in an Old-Fashioned.

Although Dutch genever is no longer widely drunk except in Dutch "brown cafes", there are still over 200 brands on the market, including fruit-flavoured ones. Many are very localized – made locally and sold in the local pub. The market is dominated by 15 major producers, of whom the largest are De Kuypers, Bols and Heineken.

FRUIT GINS

In the 19th century all the traditional distillers made a vast range of fruit-flavoured gins – orange, lemon, ginger, lovage, raspberry, damson, blackcurrant, greengage and sloe amongst them. Although many commercially produced fruit gins disappeared in the 1950s, they are back, and today one sees a large array of fruit gins available especially from smaller rural producers.

Sloe gin never went away. Described as a "British liqueur", it's made by steeping wild sloe berries, the fruit of the blackthorn tree, in gin and allowing the flavours to marry. Once the favourite drink of prim Victorian ladies and the tweed-clad, sloe gin has made the leap from the hip flasks of the hunting, shooting and fishing set to

the backs of the most stylish bars. There's now a raft of new ways of drinking sloe gin in cocktails and long drinks that tie in with the fashion for drinking seasonally, using locally sourced ingredients. Try it with English apple juice, garnished with an apple slice. Or add 25 ml of sloe gin to Champagne or sparkling wine for an apéritif that not only tastes great but also looks very pretty. Sloe gin is also delicious on its own: an excellent alternative to brandy or port as an after-dinner drink.

Both Gordon's and Plymouth make sloe gin. Another traditional brand, Hawker's Sloe Gin, has come back into production and many farm shops have also got in on the act, producing excellent sloe gins. However, sloe gin is easy to make at home.

Gather your sloe berries in the autumn after the first frosts. Fill a gin bottle halfway with sloes, add two inches of caster sugar and top up with full-strength gin. Leave for several weeks to mature. Shake the bottle every now and again, if you remember, and there it is.

FRUIT CUPS

The first and the original Pimm's No. 1 Fruit Cup was invented by James Pimm in London in 1840. He owned a chain of restaurants all over the City and made a proto-alcopop by blending gin with liqueurs, herbs and spices that he then sold to his customers in pint tankards. In 1859, he started bottling it for sale to other bars and restaurants. The company was sold to Sir Horatio Davis, a city entrepreneur, who developed an export trade for Pimm's. One of the first-recorded shipments was to the famous Galle Face Hotel in Colombo, Sri Lanka. Pimm's was also sent up the Nile, in 1898, to the forces at Khartoum and Omdurman in the Sudan.

Other Pimm's cups were introduced, based on Scotch (No. 2), brandy (No. 3), rum (No. 4), rye whisky (No. 5) and vodka (No. 6). But the first sip of the gin-based Pimm's No. 1 is still the harbinger of English summer.

GINEBRA SAN MIGUEL

Ginebra San Miguel is made in the Philippines and it is by far the biggest-selling gin brand in the world. If you ever come across it, you will wonder why: it tastes of kerosene flavoured with pine lavatory cleaner. It's bottled at 40% in small beer bottles and its massive sales reflect the fact that, outside the Muslim areas in the south, Filipino social life revolves around drinking San Miguel. Since the Philippines is one of the most populous countries in the world it's easy to see how they get through so much.

DRINKING GIN

———◆———

There are hundreds of ways to drink gin, ranging from the greatest cocktail of all time, the Dry Martini, to the *kopstet* (literally a blow to the head) – the Dutch habit of drinking genever with a half pint of lager and considered the ultimate hangover cure. In reality, the way most people encounter gin is via a Gin and Tonic,

HISTORY IN A GLASS

OPPOSITE: *Also known as the fever-tree or Jesuit's Bark,* cinchona officinalis *grows wild in the rainforests of South America, especially in Bolivia and Peru. The story of how its bark came to be a lifesaver for European colonists is a story of adventure and obsession equal to anything one might see in films like* The Raiders of the Lost Ark.

Gin and tonic water is one of those combinations that seem made for each other, the clean taste of the gin enhancing the aromatic bitterness of the tonic in a drink that is subtle, refreshing and quintessentially British. And, like other well-loved institutions – tea, suburban bungalows, pyjamas and kedgeree – Gin and Tonic owes its existence to the British presence in India.

Like gin, tonic water began life as a medicine. Its principal flavour is derived from quinine, which in turn is derived from the bark of a magical tree, *cinchona officinalis*, that grew in South America. In the 16th century Spanish colonialists found native healers using this bark as a cure for fever, particularly malaria, and began using it themselves calling it cinchona or Jesuit's Bark. Quinine is a wonder drug in that it not only calms the fever and shivering associated with malaria but also kills the parasite that causes the disease so it can be used as both a cure and a preventative treatment. In fact it is one of the most effective drugs ever known to man – Winston Churchill once attributed it with saving "more Englishmen's lives, and minds, than all the doctors in the Empire'.

Spanish Jesuit missionaries sent supplies back home to headquarters in Rome, a city particularly prone to outbreaks of malaria because of its marshy terrain. Jesuits promoted the use of the new wonder drug – hence the term Jesuit's Bark – but unfortunately that caused it to be viewed with the utmost suspicion by northern European Protestant nations who particularly hated the Jesuits. Doctors in Holland, Germany and England actively rejected the idea of any cure coming from this source.

The fame of Jesuit's Bark spread when Charles II of England was cured of malaria by a notorious quack, Robert Talbot, using the Jesuit's Bark powder mixed with wine. Charles appointed Talbot his personal physician and sent him to the French court where he proceeded to cure the king of France's son too. Talbot, despite his lack of medical training, managed to do what no one else had, and that is to understand how the bark should be administered. Crucially he discovered that quinine alkaloids were highly soluble in alcohol – so wine, not water, was the ideal medium for extracting them.

QUINQUINA GRIS.

OPPOSITE: *Sir Robert Talbot, despite his lack of medical training and to the fury of the medical establishment, was the only person in 17th-century Europe who actually understood the properties of the wonder drug for treating malaria, quinine.*

By the end of the 17th century cinchona bark was widely accepted throughout Europe as a treatment for malaria. But it was wildly expensive and varied hugely in quality, with some bark having no medicinal effect at all. Nobody knew why this was so. Over the next 150 years many expeditions were sent secretly to South America to find out more about the cinchona tree.

Slowly there developed a scientific understanding of how quinine worked, which species of tree was the best source, how it could be processed efficiently and what the correct dosages were.

By the end of the 18th century the British Navy was issuing its sailors with wine-based quinine tonics. In the 1840s British soldiers and colonials in India were using 700 tons of cinchona bark every year and in 1848 quinine extracts were added to the military and naval daily rum ration. For countries with far-flung empires, quinine was a vital necessity. The race was on to break the Spanish monopoly on the precious bark and secure their own sources.

In the 1850s British and Dutch explorers began to smuggle seeds out of Latin America and planted cinchona trees in their tropical colonies – the British in India and Ceylon (now Sri Lanka). Unfortunately they did not produce the quality of quinine necessary. Finally the Dutch successfully established plantations in Java with seeds taken from Bolivia and these did produce the required standard of quinine. By 1918 the Dutch controlled the world's supply.

In British India the bitter flavour of the daily dose of quinine was made palatable by adding sugar and diluting the mixture with soda water. And here's where the other half of the perfect combination comes into play. The British had always used gin as trade goods in India. Gin was very much part of the British way of life in the Raj, part memory of "home" and all things British, part consolation, part indulgence. It wasn't long before someone had the bright idea that gin would enliven the quinine mixture. And so the perfect sundowner was born.

Returning expats brought the taste for this exotic, bitter drink home with them. Surprisingly, because one tends to think of proprietary bottled drinks as modern, commercial production of what were called "Tonic Brewed Drinks" began as long ago as the mid-19th century. In 1858, Erasmus Bond patented "an improved aerated tonic liquid" specifying the use of quinine

THE
ENGLISH REMEDY:
OR,
ALBOR's
WONDERFUL SECRET,

FOR
C U R E I N G
O F
Agues and Feavers.
S O L D

By the Author Sir *Robert Talbor*, to the most Christian King, and since his Death, ordered by his Majesty to be Published in *French*, for the Benefit of his Subjects.

AND NOW

𝔗𝔯𝔞𝔫𝔰𝔩𝔞𝔱𝔢𝔡 𝔦𝔫𝔱𝔬 𝔈𝔫𝔤𝔩𝔦𝔰𝔥 𝔣𝔬𝔯 𝔓𝔲𝔟𝔩𝔦𝔠𝔨 𝔊𝔬𝔬𝔡.

LONDON:

Printed by *J. Wallis*, for *Jos. Hindmarsh*, at the Black Bull in *Cornhill*. MDCLXXXII.

BELOW: *Fever-Tree*
Tonic Water is one
of the new wave of
premium mixers that
uses natural quinine
grown in Africa and
other natural botanical
ingredients.

and other flavouring agents including bitter orange. Soon there were many brands of tonic water on the market with Schweppes adding Indian tonic water to its range in the 1870s.

The Dutch dominated the quinine trade until the Second World War when the Japanese occupied Java. The resulting shortage of quinine fuelled the drive to develop a synthetic version of the alkaloid. By 1944 scientists had synthesized quinine and pharmaceutical companies were able to produce various quinine-based drugs. At the same time plantations of natural cinchona were successfully established in parts of Africa.

Most modern commercially produced tonic waters are based on synthetic quinine and hence taste quite different to the original Indian tonic water, particularly in the US where tonic water tends to be much sweeter and often contains the dreaded high fructose corn syrup. There's been a bit of a backlash against this and over the past few years many excellent authentic tonic waters that do contain natural quinine and, like the original tonic waters, other botanical ingredients, have come onto the market. In the UK the best are Fentimans, Fever-Tree, Bramley & Gage and Waitrose own brand.

GIN AND TONIC

The Gin and Tonic is a great British invention that has now taken over the world. The USA and Japan were amongst the last countries to fall under its spell mostly because in both places the tonic water left a lot to be desired. However Spain is GinTonic heaven and, throughout the rest of Continental Europe, the Gin and Tonic is pretty much the gin signature serve.

A properly made Gin and Tonic is one of life's great pleasures. And although it's simple to make, use a few basic rules and one ends up with a drink that approaches perfection.

- Always use a good-quality gin.
- Use a single-serve bottle or can of tonic water.
- Take a tall glass with a heavy bottom. Fill it with ice (at least four large cubes) and add a generous measure of gin. Pour in enough tonic to fill the glass. What you're aiming for is just over double the amount of tonic to gin.
- Add a freshly cut wedge of lemon, lime or grapefruit and rub it around the rim of the glass first. Or with some very citrussy gins you can skip the extra citrus. Stir gently with a teaspoon or a cocktail stirrer.

The point about a Gin and Tonic is that it is the perfect early-evening drink. In fact the same is true of all gin-based drinks. They allow one to pass those potentially anxious hours between work and dinner at peace with the world and with oneself. Partly this is physiological – of all the common liquors gin gives the quickest lift. Partly it is psychological – gin has been associated with the hours of ease at the end of the day for a century or more.

Strange as it may seem, some people claim not to like gin. The truth is they probably don't like the taste of tonic water, which can be a Marmite-style "love it or loathe it" flavour. No problem: other mixers that work well in gin are cranberry juice, ginger ale, elderflower tonics, natural lemonade and even Appletiser. And, not to be forgotten, bitter lemon, a mixer that was common 50 years ago but has slightly fallen out of fashion. Commercial bitter lemon is tonic water with the addition of lemon juice and peel, and whilst Schweppes is the standard there are now boutique versions available from smaller producers like Fever-Tree and Fentimans.

THE DRY MARTINI

Only one thing can be said about the Dry Martini without venturing into a minefield: it is American, and, as the humorist H. L. Mencken said, "the only American invention as perfect as the sonnet". There are many conflicting stories concerning its origins. The most credible theory is proposed by drinks historians Anastasia Miller and Jared Brown who date the popularity of the mix of gin and dry (aka white) vermouth to the turn of the 20th century when the Italian Martini company was promoting heavily its new "Extra Dry Vermouth". It seems more than likely therefore that the drink took its name from the brand.

There is a fashion for calling any drink served in a Martini glass a Dry Martini. Ignore it. A proper Dry Martini is made with premium gin and French vermouth. There has always been much argument as to the correct way to make it. At one end of the divide are those who advocate a standard 4:1 gin-to-vermouth ratio. At the other are Martini aficionados like the filmmaker Luis Bunuel who advised "simply allowing a ray of sunlight to shine through a bottle of Noilly Prat before it hits the bottle of gin". Winston Churchill apparently just bowed in the direction of France as he measured his Plymouth Gin into a glass with an olive.

One hesitates to stick one's head over the parapet but what should be considered is, at what point is the Dry Martini still a cocktail and not just a glass of cold neat gin with a spray of lemon juice? For my money that point is reached when it's made the "in and out" way:

Into a cold metal shaker filled with ice pour one tablespoon of dry vermouth to coat the ice. Strain off the excess vermouth and pour in 210 ml of gin. Stir until ice-cold, and then strain into two cold cocktail glasses. Either zest the oil from two strips of lemon peel over each glass or garnish each drink with a single olive. A small, pickled cocktail onion makes it a Gibson. Notice the Martini here is stirred not shaken: science tells us to shake a drink when you want it colder and slightly more diluted, stir when you want more flavour.

There are variations of the Dry Martini that still preserve the integrity of the recipe. The Smoky Martini for example adds a

THE BOMBAY SAPPHIRE MARTINI. AS BALANCED BY HILTON McCONNICO.

POUR SOMETHING PRICELESS

Bombay Sapphire™ Gin 47% alc./vol. (94 Proof). 100% neutral spirits. ©1997 Carillon Importers LTD., Teaneck, NJ. ©1997 Hilton McConnico.

spoonful of malt whisky floated over the top, the Dirty Martini a splash of olive brine. The Cajun Martini mixes gin infused with jalapeno chillies with dry vermouth and a pepper garnish.

The other main ingredient of the Martini is vermouth – from the German "wermut", the name of its principal flavouring,

ABOVE: This Bombay Sapphire advertisement highlighted the sophistication of the Martini.

wormwood. Vermouth is white wine, blended, fortified and made aromatic through the addition of macerated herbs and spices, chiefly the flowers of wormwood (its leaves are used to make absinthe). There are three kinds of vermouth: Italian such as Martini & Rossi and Cinzano; Savoie; and southern French, typically Noilly Prat that is the best for Dry Martinis.

Ask for a Dry Martini in a bar and the bartender will practically hug you as mixing the drink is the ultimate test of cocktail craft and everyone has his or her own particular trick. It's also a bit of a test of drinking skill and should be approached with caution. As the old joke goes, "the Martini is like a woman's breasts because one is not enough and three's too many". Or, as Dorothy Parker put it:

"I like to have a Martini
Two at the very most
After three I'm under the table
After four I'm under the host"

Of all gin long drinks the Collins is the most versatile and its basic combination of gin, sugar syrup, lemon juice and soda water can be played around with endlessly to reflect the taste profiles of different gins and to accommodate seasonal flavours. The beauty of the Collins is that its ingredients are simple and found in every kitchen. It's also a good alternative for those who find the taste of tonic water overpowering.

TOM COLLINS

50 ml gin
Juice of half a lemon
100 ml soda water
2 tsp caster sugar
Wedge of fresh lemon

ABOVE: *The Tom Collins cocktail is easy to create and its history can be traced back to "Professor" Jerry Thomas in the 1870s.*

Add the lemon juice and sugar to a tall glass and stir until the sugar has dissolved. Add the gin then fill the glass with ice and stir. Top up with soda water and stir carefully once more. Garnish with one fresh lemon wedge.

Making sugar syrup, which many classic cocktail recipes call for, is easy. In a saucepan combine 250g caster sugar with 250 ml water. Bring to the boil, stirring, until sugar has dissolved. Allow to cool. Or if time is short just dissolve two teaspoons of caster sugar in two teaspoons of water.

CRIMSON FIZZ

50 ml gin
1 tablespoon sugar syrup
6 strawberries

Crush the strawberries and shake with the gin and sugar syrup for several minutes, then strain into a cold tall glass. Fizz up with bottled soda water, stirring continuously as water is added. The point of this drink is that it should be served foaming.

ELDERFLOWER COLLINS

50 ml gin
50 ml lemon juice
12.5 ml elderflower cordial
12.5 ml shot sugar syrup

Build in the glass, stirring well. Fizz up with bottled soda water, stirring continuously as water is added. Add ice. Delicious on a summer's day.

The Gin Rickey is first cousin to a Collins but is made with fresh lime juice rather than lemon juice and with no sugar. It can be traced to Shoemakers Restaurant in Washington where a bartender invented the drink in the early years of the 20th century. The first person to try it was a Colonel Jim Rickey, hence the name.

BELOW: *The peach and elderflower Collins is just part of the Collins family of cocktails.*

PEACH AND ELDERFLOWER COLLINS

50 ml gin
25 ml freshly squeezed lemon juice
15 ml elderflower cordial
One third of a fresh white peach, diced or
20 ml of good-quality white peach puree
50 ml soda water

Muddle the diced white peach in the bottom of a clean highball glass. Add the fresh lemon juice, elderflower cordial and gin. Stir well. Add plenty of cubed ice. Stir again. Top with soda water then stir for a final time to chill and combine all of the ingredients. Garnish with a clear straw and a wedge of white peach.

PINK GIN

"Pinkers" – as it is known amongst sailors – is a very British drink that came into being courtesy of the Royal Navy. A Navy ship's surgeon first used a combination of Angostura bitters, gin and a splash of water as a cure for seasickness during long sea voyages and the drink caught on. In former British colonies Pink Gin was known as Gin Pahit (Pahit mans bitter in Malay) and the addition of tiny onions marinated in chilli makes it a Gin Piaj. Whatever its name, drinking this drink once instantly identified you as a navy man or a colonial. It's not a drink for the faint-hearted.

2 dashes Angostura bitters
1 part gin
1 part water

Swirl several drops of Angostura bitters around in a short glass. Shake out the residue and add the gin and water. No ice. Remember: it's British.

THE GIMLET

The super-simple combination of gin and Rose's Lime Juice also has a strong connection to the Royal Navy and dates back to 1867 when Lachlan Rose, a Scottish chandler based in Edinburgh, came up with a formula to preserve citrus fruit juice without using alcohol. It was desperately needed because scurvy, caused by a deficiency of vitamin C, was still a major danger for sailors on long sea voyages. With superb timing, that same year a law required all vessels, Royal Navy and Merchant, to carry limes, not lemons, to be given daily to the crews. This led to the remarkable success of Rose's Lime Juice and along the way resulted in British sailors being called "limeys".

Dr Gimlette, a British naval surgeon, reputedly invented the drink that was then named after him. Here's the recipe:

1 part gin
1 part Rose's Lime Juice (it doesn't work with fresh lime juice)

Pour ingredients into a mixing glass three-quarters filled with ice cubes. Stir until ice-cold. Strain into a chilled Martini glass. Garnish with a slice of lime peel.

BELOW: *Another simple gin cocktail is the Gimlet; just gin and lime juice, but not freshly squeezed lime.*

OTHER CLASSIC COCKTAILS

THE WHITE LADY

Invented in the 1920s by Scottish bartender Harry MacElhone, initially at Ciro's. Later perfected at the famous Harry's New York Bar in Paris in 1929.

50 ml gin
19 ml Cointreau
19 ml freshly squeezed lemon juice
6 ml sugar syrup
$^{1}/_{2}$ egg white

Shake with ice, strain into a chilled Martini glass and garnish with a lemon twist.

For a Clover Club add 25 ml of raspberry syrup.

The Negroni is the most perfect gin aperitif, one that real gin lovers love. It's also a drink whose provenance can be traced to a specific time and place. Imagine the scene: the Bar Casoni in Florence, circa 1920, where patrons are enjoying their Americanos, a drink made with Campari, sweet vermouth and soda water, named thus because of pro-American feelings after World War I. But one regular had his own ideas: every day, Count Camillo Negroni ordered his Americano to be made with gin and without soda water. Soon his friends began to request their drinks "the Negroni way". A classic was born.

Unlikely as it seems this story is almost certainly true. Count Negroni certainly existed. He led a colourful life, having been a cowboy and a professional gambler in the United States in his youth.

The fame of his invention spread beyond Florence and it became the favourite drink of the Italian Futurists, the avant-garde literary and artistic movement led  by Filippo Tommaso Marinetti. Along with many other gin cocktails from the great cocktail age of the 1920s, the Negroni has now become ultra-fashionable again. Partly that is to do with its authenticity, partly too because, like the Martini, it's a drinker's drink. As Kingsley Amis, one of alcohol's great heroes, said: "This is a really fine invention. It has the power, rare with drinks and indeed with anything else, of cheering you up."

The recipe could not be simpler:

Equal parts of gin, Campari and Italian red vermouth such as Martini Rosso. Combine all the ingredients in a mixing glass filled with ice. Stir gently and pour into an old-fashioned glass. Add a hefty orange slice as a garnish.

Although there is no doubt that cocktails are quintessentially American, there has always been a tradition of making mixed drinks in Britain that goes back to Victorian times. Although of course they weren't called cocktails but rather daisies, flips, fizzes, cobblers, slings, punches and many other terms.

GRAPEFRUIT GIN FIZZ

The Fizz is very much in the Collins family in that it is served in a tall glass and includes a carbonated mixer.

> *50 ml gin*
> *75 ml Ruby Grapefruit Juice*
> *Splash of Club Soda*
> *Garnish*

Pour gin into a tall glass with large cubes of ice. Add ruby grapefruit juice and top with soda water. Garnish with a wedge of ruby grapefruit.

THE MONKEY GLAND

The Monkey Gland cocktail was created in the 1920s by the famous Harry MacElhone, owner of Harry's New York Bar in Paris. The drink's name was inspired by the experiments of surgeon Serge Voronoff who had invented a technique of grafting monkey testicle tissue on to the testicles of men to boost virility.

40 ml gin
20 ml orange juice
1 teaspoon grenadine syrup
1 dash absinthe
Orange peel for garnish

Mix all ingredients in a shaker. Garnish with orange peel.

THE SIDECAR

Also known as the Chelsea Sidecar to differentiate it from the original recipe traditionally made with cognac, it is believed to have been invented around the end of World War I, in either London or Paris. The Sidecar was named for the motorcycle passenger seat. It's a kind of daisy cocktail.

50 ml gin
20 ml Triple Sec, such as Cointreau
20 ml lemon juice

Mix all the ingredients together and serve.

ABOVE: *Whether the Monkey Gland experiment worked or not, the cocktail has been popular for almost a century.*

NEW WAVE COCKTAILS

The modern craft cocktail revolution has generated some splendid new-style cocktails that make the most of fresh fruits, herbs and even vegetables.

BASIL SMASH

(If you are ever in Hamburg you will find one of the best bars in the world, Le Lion, run by Joerg Meyer who invented this delicious drink.)

60 ml gin
1 lemon
20 ml sugar syrup
6–8 large basil leaves

BELOW: *The Basil Smash is a simple mixture of lemon, sugar syrup, basil leaves and gin.*

Cut a lemon in half and squeeze the juice into a shaker. Throw in the squeezed lemon as well. Add basil leaves and muddle. Fill the shaker with ice cubes. Shake vigorously. Strain into a tumbler filled with fresh ice.

THE BRAMBLE

(Invented by Dick Bradsell, a pioneer of the London craft cocktail movement.)

50 ml gin
25 ml freshly squeezed lemon juice
12.5 ml shot sugar syrup
12.5 ml shot crème de mure

Shake the first three ingredients over ice and strain into an old-fashioned glass filled with crushed ice. Slowly drizzle the crème de mure through the crushed ice to create a "marbled" effect and garnish with blackberries and a lemon slice.

EARL GREY MARTEAINI

(The creation of Audrey Saunders, the first lady of American cocktails.)

45 ml Earl Grey tea-infused gin
25 ml freshly squeezed lemon juice
30 ml simple syrup
1 egg white

Shake ingredients hard for 10 seconds. Strain into a chilled cocktail glass that is half-rimmed with sugar. Garnish with a lemon twist.

For the Earl Grey infusion, measure four tablespoons of loose Earl Grey tea into a litre bottle of gin. Cap and shake, and leave for two hours. Strain through a fine sieve into a bowl. Rinse out bottle to remove loose tea, and pour infusion back into clean bottle.

ABOVE: *Earl Grey tea has the aroma of bergamot, a botanical sometimes used in the distillation of gin.*

190 ROYALE

This is a version of the old standard Sloe Royale.

50 ml gin
25 ml sloe gin
Mint leaves
2 wedges lime
Sugar syrup
25 ml fresh lemon juice
Champagne or Prosecco

Take a few mint leaves and the lime wedges, and muddle with a dash of sugar syrup. Add the lemon juice, and top up with crushed ice. Add the gin and sloe gin, then stir. Top with Champagne or Prosecco and serve in a Collins glass.

LEFT: *The 190 Royale, a sparkling cocktail with a fresh, fruity taste.*

PUNCHES AND SHARING DRINKS

Punch, a very Victorian drink immortalized by Charles Dickens, has recently made a comeback, particularly during the winter months when nothing is quite as comforting as a bowl of sweet, fragrant, alcohol-infused cheer. As Dickens writes in *David Copperfield*, even the task of making punch is a pleasure.

"Punch, my dear Copperfield, like time and tide, waits for no man … His recent despondency, not to say despair, was gone in a moment. I never saw a man so thoroughly enjoy himself amid the fragrance of lemon-peel and sugar, the odour of burning spirit, and the steam of boiling water, as Mr Micawber did that afternoon. It was wonderful to see his face shining at us out of a thin cloud of these delicate fumes, as he stirred, and mixed, and tasted, and looked as if he were making, instead of a punch, a fortune for his family down to the latest posterity."

DICKENSIAN PUNCH

The word "punch" comes from the Sanskrit for "five" as the drink was originally made with five ingredients: alcohol, sugar, lemon, water, and tea or spices. Punch was introduced to England by sailors and employees of the British East India Company in the early 17th century. It was a popular drink in Victorian times and was by all accounts a drink that the great chronicler of the Victorian age, Charles Dickens, himself took great pleasure in making and serving at home.

> *150 ml gin*
> *1 litre of good-quality hoppy ale*
> *200 ml cloudy apple juice*
> *5 slices of satsuma*
> *1 cinnamon stick*
> *90g sugar*
> *5g hops*
> *2 cloves*
> *1 dessert spoon honey*
> *2 large splashes of Angostura Bitters*
> *1 whole star anise*

Heat ingredients all in a pan. Simmer for 20 minutes then strain the hops out and serve with satsuma slices and a stick of cinnamon to garnish. For six people.

ARIZONA BREEZE

Making cocktails at home for a crowd can be time-consuming but drinks like the gin version of the Sea Breeze can easily be made up in quantities.

> *65 ml gin*
> *75 ml cranberry juice*
> *50 ml grapefruit juice*

These basic proportions can be used to make a jug of ready-to-serve cocktails by multiplying as necessary. Add ice to glasses as you serve.

SUMMER COOLER

Based on jug serving six medium tumblers.

> *200 ml gin*
> *75 ml of elderflower cordial or liqueur*
> *Club soda or ginger ale*
> *Lemon*
> *Garnish: summer fruits*

Pour gin over ice into the pitcher. Add the elderflower cordial or liqueur. Top with club soda or ginger ale and garnish with a squeeze of lemon and summer fruits.

GIN PLACES

Until recently, if you wanted to see gin being made and explore its fascinating history in detail, the options were limited. Now, however, no matter where you are, you won't be far from a distillery visitor centre where you can enjoy tours and tastings and, in some cases, even make your own gin.

- BEEFEATER DISTILLERY AND VISITOR CENTRE:
  20 Montford Place, London SE11 5DE.
  Book online at www.beefeatervisitorcentre.co.uk

- THE BOMBAY SAPPHIRE DISTILLERY:
  Laverstoke Mill, Laverstoke, Whitchurch,
  Hampshire RG28 7NR.
  Visit www.bombaysapphire.com to buy experience
  and event tickets online

- CITY OF LONDON DISTILLERY:
  22–24 Bride Lane, London EC4Y 8DT.
  For bookings http://cityoflondondistillery.com/

- SIPSMITH DISTILLERY:
  83 Cranbrook Road, London W4 2LJ.
  Book at www.sipsmith.com

- THE GINSTITUTE:
  The Portobello Star, 171 Portobello Road,
  London W11 2DY.
  Book at http://portobellostarbar.co.uk/ginstitu-
  telondon/

- THE LONDON DISTILLERY COMPANY:
  33 Parkgate Road, London SW11 4NP.
  Contact: hi@londondistillery.com

- PICKERING'S GIN:
  Summerhall Distillery, Summerhall Place,
  Edinburgh EH9 1QH.
  Book at http://www.pickeringsgin.com/

- PLYMOUTH GIN DISTILLERY:
  60 Southside Street, The Barbican,
  Plymouth, Devon PL1 2LQ.
  Book at http://booking.plymouthgin.com/
  distillery-tours/cat_5.html

- MUSEUM OF JENEVER:
  Lange Haven 74–76,
  3111 CH Schiedam,
  Netherlands.
  Tel: +31 10 246 9676

- HOUSE OF BOLS COCKTAIL
  & GENEVER EXPERIENCE:
  Paulus Potterstraat 14,
  1070 CZ Amsterdam, Netherlands.
  Tel: +31 20 570 8575

INDEX

GERALDINE COATES is a professional writer and editor who specialises in writing about the world of drinks, in particular spirits. She has written regularly for a number of newspapers, including *The Glasgow Herald*, *The Scotsman*, *Scotland on Sunday* and *The Sunday Times Scotland*. As an author, she wrote *The Mixellany Guide to Gin*, *Discovering Gin* and contributed to *The Mitchell Beazley Pocket Whisky Book* and *The Taste of Scotland Guide*.

PICTURE CREDITS

The publishers would like to thank the following sources for their kind permission to reproduce the pictures in this book.

Advertising Archives: 34; **Alamy:** /The Art Archive: 163; /Marc Hill: 87; /Newscast: 112B; **Anchor Distilling Company:** 127; **BB&R Spirits Limited:** 132L; **Bacardi:** 134; **Beam Suntory Inc.:** 128; **Beefeater:** 88, 94, 95, 97; **Bermondsey Gin:** 126; **Black Forest Distillers GmbH:** 131R; **Bluecoat American Dry Gin:** 99R; **Bombay Sapphire:** 23, 85, 89, 100, 102, 172, 175; **Boodles Gin:** 103; **Gabriel Boudier Dijon:** 106; **Bramley and Gage Ltd:** 141; **Broker's Gin:** 107; **Bruichladdich:** 146, 147; **Bulldog Gin:** 107L; **Burnett's White Satin:** 108; **Caorunn Gin:** 110; **City of London Distillery:** 112T; **Cognac Ferrand:** 111; **Corbis:** /Jens Kalaene/dpa: 64-65; **Death's Door Spirits:** 114L; **Diageo:** 144, 145, 158; **Distillery No.209:** 132R; **Exact PR:** 123, 124; **Fever-Tree:** 166-167; **Fifty Pounds Gin:** 116L; **Fords Gin:** 116R; **Foxdenton Estate Company Ltd:** 117; **G'Vine:** 122; **Getty Images:** /Spencer Arnold: 8; /Steve Brown Photography: 183T; /Guildhall Library & Art Gallery/Heritage Images: 18-19, 31; /Hulton Archive: 160; /Popperfoto: 62; /The Print Collector: 61, 105; /Chris Ratcliffe/Bloomberg: 74-75; /Oli Scarff: 60; /Underwood Archives: 63; **Gin Mare:** 119; **Graphic Bar, London:** 92; **Greenalls:** 70-71, 86; **Halewood International:** 150; **Hendrick's Gin:** 125; **The London Distillery Company:** 114R; **Lucas Bols:** 156-157; **Ian Macleod Distillers Ltd:** 129; **Mary Evans Picture Library:** 14-15, 22, 37, 38-39, 43, 47, 48-49; **Park Place Drinks:** 143; **Pickering's Gin:** 135; **Plymouth Gin:** 137, 178; **Portobello Road Gin:** 6, 52, 138T, 138B; **Private Collection:** 10, 11, 13, 17, 24-25, 26, 29, 45, 68-69, 76, 118, 171, 180, 181, 183B, 185; **Quintessential Brands UK Holdings Limited:** 98, 99L, 121, 133, 179; **Reformed Spirits Company Ltd:** 130, 131L; **Rex Features:** /Everett Collection: 173; **Richmond Towers Communications:** 153; **Sacred:** 139; **Shutterstock:** 66, 120, 169, 174; **Sipsmith:** 140; **The Spencerfield Spirit Company Ltd:** 115; **Steely Fox:** 177, 182; **Toorank UK Ltd:** 142; **United Distillers and Vintners Archive, Leven:** 41, 50, 51, 54, 57, 58, 59, 78, 80, 83, 90-91; **Vin Mag Archive:** 56; **Voice PR:** 148; **Eric Weller:** 46; **WM Cadenhead Ltd:** 109; **Warner Edwards:** 149, 154; **Wemyss Malts:** 113; **Wikimedia Commons:** 20, 33, 55, 73, 165; **Zuidam Distillers:** 151

Every effort has been made to acknowledge correctly and contact the source and/or copyright holder of each picture and Carlton Books Limited apologises for any unintentional errors or omissions that will be corrected in future editions of this book.